ROUTLEDGE LIBRARY EDITIONS:
BANKING & FINANCE

THE BANKING CRISIS

THE BANKING CRISIS

The End of an Epoch

MARCUS NADLER AND JULES I. BOGEN

Volume 24

Routledge
Taylor & Francis Group
LONDON AND NEW YORK

First published in the UK in 1934

This edition first published in 2012
by Routledge
2 Park Square, Milton Park, Abingdon, Oxon, OX14 4RN

Simultaneously published in the USA and Canada
by Routledge
711 Third Avenue, New York, NY 10017

Routledge is an imprint of the Taylor & Francis Group, an informa business

British Library Cataloguing in Publication Data
A catalogue record for this book is available from the British Library

ISBN: 978-0-415-52086-7 (Set)
eISBN: 978-0-203-10819-2 (Set)
ISBN: 978-0-415-52812-2 (Volume 24)
eISBN: 978-0-203-11683-8 (Volume 24)

Publisher's Note
The publisher has gone to great lengths to ensure the quality of this reprint but points out that some imperfections in the original copies may be apparent.

THE BANKING CRISIS

The End of an Epoch

BY

MARCUS NADLER

AND

JULES I. BOGEN

LONDON
GEORGE ALLEN & UNWIN LTD
MUSEUM STREET

BROUGHT UP TO DATE AND PUBLISHED
IN GREAT BRITAIN WITH NEW
MATERIAL 1934

PRINTED IN GREAT BRITAIN BY
HENDERSON AND SPALDING LTD LONDON SE15

To

John T. Madden

PREFACE

The closing of the banks throughout the United States on March 6 was a seven days' wonder throughout the world. From the rivers to the ends of the Earth, the collapse of the banking system of a nation that had attained an industrial, commercial and financial development never even approached in all the previous history of Mankind caused astonishment and shock.

Was this collapse inevitable, or did it represent merely an effect of a world-wide depression in which the United States was a helpless but innocent victim. In the following pages, we seek to give a specific answer to this fundamental question by tracing post-war economic history and its relations to the American banking system.

Our aim is first to present a clear, simple and concise explanation of why the American banking crisis of 1933 occurred. The bulk of the volume is devoted to an analytical narrative of the actual events of the final major panic which was ushered in by the closing down of the banks in the State of Michigan on February 14, 1933. The three following weeks made history. Events then came so thick and fast that years of banking history seemed to have been compressed into as many days. The effort is here made to disentangle the important from the ephemeral, so that the reader can view what has happened from the vantage point afforded by considering the panic in relation to what came before. The scholar and the pedant will later go over this same ground in far greater detail than has been possible or desirable to writers who seek to analyze events that, figuratively speaking, happened "only yesterday."

In the closing chapter, we outline the legislative steps which we regard as necessary for a permanent reform of the American system, so that what happened in 1933 shall not happen again.

The authors wish to acknowledge the whole-hearted aid given them in the preparation of the manuscript by Dean A. Wellington Taylor of the Graduate School of Business Administration of New York University; Dr. Sipa Heller, Mr. Harry Sauvain, and Mr. Frank Dow, of New York University.

CONTENTS

CHAPTER I.—THE STAGE IS SET, 1919–1929

A FATEFUL WEEK

ON the night of Sunday, March 5, 1933, the pomp and circumstance of Inauguration Day still ringing in his ears, President Franklin D. Roosevelt issued a proclamation closing all the banks of the country and placing an embargo on gold exports. This step, unprecedented in this country in time of peace, was taken by the President under the Trading with the Enemy Act, which was resurrected from the dust-laden archives of dead statutes. It was needed to permit the country to face a financial squall which, after hovering over us for three years, finally struck with terrific and overpowering force at the very moment that a change in the government was taking place.

During the following week, the financial machinery of the country was all but completely shut down. After having developed the habit, over a period of several decades, of utilizing bank checks as the ordinary medium of exchange for some 90 per cent of all its business transactions, the American public suddenly found itself without banks. The wheels of trade and industry slowed down immediately and a complete paralysis of the economic life of the nation was threatened.

The new Administration, after a trying period of hesitation and conflicting counsels, struck out vigorously with a series of decisive measures which permitted a reopening of most banks during the following week. On March 9, a special session of Congress rushed through a comprehensive banking bill within the record time of 7½ hours. On March 11, President Roosevelt in a new proclamation, one of many issued during a fateful week in which the country was run by executive decree along lines made familiar in Russia and Germany, announced that the machinery had been perfected for a full reopening of "sound banks."

The momentous week of the banking panic marked the end of an epoch in American finance. It also witnessed the end of a system—the post-war system, the failure of which was characterized by the Great Depression ushered in by the stock market panic of 1929. We are concerned in this chapter with the major features of the economic system of the decade of the Twenties, whose end was signalized first by the stock market panic of 1929, but more finally and completely by the banking panic of 1933.

THE EVILS OF THE PEACE

The banking collapse of 1933 in the United States marked the culmination of one of the most dramatic and moving chapters in the history of modern capitalism. It came as the climax of a series of episodes that followed each other with startling inevitability. Like the grim tragedies of Æschylus or the Book of Job, disaster followed disaster in unerring fashion, so that the final catastrophe, we can see in retrospect, was inescapable.

When fighting his losing battle to retain the Presidency in 1932, Herbert Hoover blamed the financial and economic difficulties which beset his Administration on the World War. Unquestionably, that Armageddon caused vast losses in men and material things. But there can be no denial of the fact that the war witnessed a great stimulation of productive activity and inventive genius on the part of the nations of the West. The United States in particular enjoyed a rate of economic progress through the years of the conflict it had seldom if ever attained before. True, the financing of our participation in the war was accomplished in the main through the sale of some $20,000,000,000 in government obligations, but this involved no net cost of itself to the country. It merely resulted in our own citizens becoming creditors of the government to this vast amount, with the banks, directly through investments and indirectly through loans, furnishing the credit to make sales of the enormous Liberty bond issues possible.

The great inflation of bank credit through the war years, facilitated in large measure through the newly organized Federal Reserve banks, was one result of the war which contained the seeds of later disaster. As we shall see, however, the seeds thus planted during the war years were to account for only a small fraction of the later crop of financial troubles. The planting of wild oats was to be resumed on a much broader scale once the conflict was ended.

Herbert Hoover blamed the depression of the Thirties upon the World War. He would have been more correct if he had placed the blame rather upon the Peace which followed. Whom the Gods would destroy they first make mad, the old Latin proverb states. Historians of the future will point out that the Great War gave birth to a generation of political leaders who were veritable economic and financial madmen.

President Wilson, in his famous fourteen points, showed the way to a sane peace. But the Treaty of Versailles and the subsequent arrangements made to restore peace in Europe and elsewhere were the work of madmen. The map of Europe was redrawn to aggrandize the victor and weaken the vanquished, with a number of new states created for purposes military or expedient, with little or no regard to economic consequences. Reparations and war debts were to be collected without reference to the very simple economic truth that payments between nations in the long run can be settled only in goods, services or gold. Nations new and old then proceeded to pile tariff barrier on tariff barrier, so that international trade was deflected and diverted from normal channels and the very basis for any international debt payments undermined.

Through it all, politics dominated economics. Strangely enough, economic experts in every country lent their names and their talents to this rebuilding of the old pre-war world in topsy-turvy fashion, without warning or protest. J. Maynard Keynes, almost alone, issued Cassandra-like warnings to a world that turned deaf ears to his gloomy but unerringly true prophecies. In two trenchant volumes, "The Economic Consequences of the Peace" and "Revision of the Treaty," he pointed out the imbecility of the new economic arrangements, but his was a voice crying in the wilderness.

THE RESORT TO INFLATION

The post-war world, after Versailles, faced the necessarily painful readjustments of getting down to a peace-time basis. This process would have required several difficult years, and might well have made the post-war decade one of disturbed business and alternating periods of moderate prosperity and depression. The inept arrangements set up by the peace treaty, furthermore, would have brought about inevitably a major economic depression, which would have proved to the world the need for mending its ways and doing away with the incubus of reparations, war debts, uneconomic trade barriers, etc.

The political and financial leaders of the Twenties decided, however, that this cataclysm, this day of reckoning, inevitable though it seemed, should not occur. They turned to the antidote of inflation, of debt creation. The reason why the inevitable corrective depression of the early Twenties was postponed for a decade, with consequent manifold exaggeration of the disease, was the general resort to inflation throughout the world.

Inflation means simply an increase in the available purchasing power. The capitalistic world uses as purchasing power both metallic and paper money and credit, or promises to pay money. Such purchasing power may be said to have two dimensions—quantity and velocity of turnover. Ten dollars hoarded and unused is not actual purchasing power. When it is used in trade and commerce it becomes active purchasing power. Ten dollars used once during a year is equal, in its effect upon business and the price level, to one dollar used ten times within a similar period of time. It is a truism that every ordinary business transaction involves payment in money or bank credit instruments, so that the volume of business transactions, stated in money, at any one time will be equal to the volume of money and credit outstanding, multiplied by the average rate of turnover or velocity of such money and credit. Inflation of purchasing media, through increase in its quantity or velocity of turnover, can go on regardless of whether or not a country remains on the gold standard—that is, offers to convert its outstanding currency into gold or the equivalent.

The world of the Twenties witnessed an unprecedented resort to inflation of purchasing power as an antidote to the unbalanced economic conditions of the time. Inflation went on both nationally and internationally. The old reliance upon automatic economic adjustments, upon the *laissez-faire* doctrines preached by the British classical economists, gave way to a general recourse to currency and credit management as a means of escaping the penalties of economic maladjustments. The world sought to escape from the consequences of its economic misdeeds. It manufactured money on a huge scale to keep itself supplied with purchasing power to overcome threatened depressions. Alas, the escape was short-lived, and the final consequences far more disastrous than would have been the case without such artificial stimuli.

When once the European currencies were actually stabilized, so that the stimulus of currency inflation ceased, the poverty and destruction caused by the war and the ravages of the immediate post-war currency depreciation were revealed in a glaring light. This, however, did not deter the world. At the Genoa Conference, the gold exchange standard, which permits the use of foreign exchange as part of the reserves of a central bank and thus enables a given amount of gold to do double duty, was generally adopted. The adoption of the gold exchange standard, in turn, led to the accumulation of large volumes of foreign short-term balances and gold in the leading financial centers of the world, particularly the United States. The resultant low rates of interest in these centers created a favorable bond market and, from 1923 to the end of 1928, the billions of dollars placed by the United States abroad in the form of foreign loans, coupled with the liberal credit policies of the various central banks, created an era of artificial business activity and prosperity on a world scale. It was obvious, however, that the moment the United States would cease to pour billions of dollars abroad, this era of prosperity must come to an end.

The Great Depression of the Thirties is a world-wide phenomenon. No thinking person, however, in the light of what is known now, can say that it started in any one country or was a result of the economic policies of any one nation. Nearly all nations have suffered, and nearly all contributed their bit to the maladjustments and the inflation which made the ultimate cataclysm so inevitable and so severe. In this chapter, we shall sketch the story of Inflation in the United States.

FEDERAL RESERVE POLICIES AND INFLATION

The United States, during and after the war, was in position to inflate its available purchasing power on a scale never dreamed possible before. This was a direct result of the establishment of the Federal Reserve System. As a mere banking instrument, the system is doubtless the greatest inflation machine ever devised. Those who set it up dreamed of an efficient management for the system which would keep it under rational control, and make of it an effective stabilizing agent in our economic structure. They reckoned in terms of ratios and reserves rather than of men, however. In practice, the Federal Reserve System has worked with marvelous efficiency as an agency for credit expansion and prosperity creation but it has but seldom been utilized with any material effect to deflate credit and check speculative booms.

The primrose path of expansion and inflation has ever beckoned to those who manage the Federal Reserve System's affairs and seek to curry popular and political favor for themselves and their institutions. The thorny road of repression and deflation, so necessary at times, they have almost always strenuously avoided. At times, the Reserve System has taken steps to break a boom as it did in 1928 and 1929, but these have generally been taken late or have been offset by other acts which neutralized the deflationary measures adopted. Thus, when the Federal Reserve Bank of New York raised its rediscount rate from 5 to 6 per cent at the height of the boom in 1929, it cut the rate at which it offered to buy bankers' acceptances, an equally effective outlet for Reserve bank credit, to 5 per cent as an offset.

The inflationary possibilities of the Federal Reserve System arise from the great efficacy which it imparts to bank reserves. The Federal Reserve Act requires each member bank in the system to keep a small percentage of its deposits with the Reserve banks as a legal reserve. The New York and Chicago member banks must keep 13 per cent of their demand deposits with their Reserve banks. In 62 other so-called reserve cities, 10 per cent of demand deposits must be kept as reserves with the Federal Reserve banks. In other communities, the so-called country banks must keep 7 per cent reserves against demand deposits. Time deposits, on which the banks may require notice before withdrawal, carry a required reserve of only 3 per cent.

Under the old National Banking System, much larger reserves had to be kept on hand, and the reserves in the form of gold or currency had to be kept partly in the banks' own vaults and partly in the vaults of other institutions. The central reserve city banks had to keep a 25 per cent monetary reserve against deposits entirely in cash in their own vaults. The Federal Reserve System introduced vast inflationary possibilities, however, not only because it cut down reserves sharply, but also because it was required that all reserves be kept in the Federal Reserve banks, which could then provide additional reserve funds to individual member banks by giving them the privilege of rediscounting. Thus, member banks felt freer than ever to expand their loans and investments, knowing full well that whenever needed they could obtain additional reserve funds from the Federal Reserve banks. By pooling the banking reserves of the country with the Reserve banks and making them available for lending back to the member banks, the Reserve System inserted vast inflationary potentialities into our banking structure.

These inflationary potentialities were further increased to an enormous degree by the powers granted the Reserve banks, both in the original act and in the so-called War Amendments of 1917, never repealed, to buy government securities and bankers' acceptances in the open market. Such open market operations, made famous since on several notable occasions, enabled the Reserve banks to manipulate the volume of available bank reserves of the country, regardless of whether the banks did or did not rediscount of their own volition.

The vast power of the Federal Reserve System arises from the fact that its activities have an influence that is magnified many-fold in terms of dollars and cents. If an individual purchases a government bond for $1,000, he merely transfers his bank deposit for that amount to the account of the seller of the bond. If a commercial bank purchases a bond for $1,000 and pays for it in the usual way by issuing a cashier's check on itself, the net effect may be to increase total outstanding bank deposits by $1,000. But when a Federal Reserve bank indulges in a so-called open market operation and purchases a $1,000 government bond from a dealer, it pays with a cashier's check on itself, so-called Federal funds. When the dealer deposits the check in his bank, the latter thus becomes possessed of new reserves.

Such an increase in available reserves permits the banks of the country to expand loans and investments an average of ten times over. Hence, the Federal Reserve banks, through manipulation of the amount of bank reserves, can and frequently do bring about a multiple expansion or contraction of member bank credit, unless general conditions are such that they dare not or cannot make their policies effective.

James W. Gerard, former ambassador to Germany, once made public a list of 49 industrialists and financiers whom he named as the men who actually control America. Stalin, Mussolini, Hitler

—these are types of political dictators endowed with vast powers. These popular heroes enjoy but limited potency, however, when their power to influence the economic life of peoples is compared with that which rested in the hands of heads of central banks during the Twenties. The central banks were able, through manipulation of open market operations and discount rates, to expand and contract entire credit systems, for a time, at will. During the Twenties, before the Great Depression set loose forces which made their efforts largely ineffective, the heads of the central banks of the United States, Great Britain, France and Germany enjoyed a measure of economic power that has perhaps never been attained by any small group of individuals before. And they decided to throw this vast power and influence into a gigantic effort to prevent the world from paying for the ravages of the war, the madness of the treaties of peace and for their own mistakes committed in connection with the attempted stabilization of currencies and credit management by central banks.

HOW THE BANKS EXPANDED CREDIT

The chief characteristics of the history of American banking during the post-war decade in which the seeds of the Great Depression were being sown, may be summarized as follows:

1. *Bank credit was expanded at a rapid pace* in the United States, with the encouragement and at times the direct stimulation of the Federal Reserve authorities.

The annual statistics tell the story. Loans and investments of all the banks in the country (as shown by the annual reports of the Comptroller of the Currency) increased as follows:

LOANS AND INVESTMENTS OF ALL BANKS IN THE UNITED STATES

(In millions of dollars)

Year (June 30)	*Loans*	*Investments*	*Total*
1919	$24,723	$11,847	$36,570
1920	30,839	10,845	41,684
1921	28,988	11,012	40,000
1922	27,750	12,206	39,956
1923	30,398	13,341	43,739
1924	31,541	13,639	45,180
1925	33,882	14,948	48,830
1926	36,176	15,386	51,562
1927	37,378	16,373	53,751
1928	39,483	17,782	57,265
1929	41,531	16,943	58,474
1930	40,638	17,471	58,109
1931	35,384	19,637	55,021

The expansion of credit which averaged 6 per cent per annum from 1919 to 1930 for commercial banks, gives concrete evidence of the steady increase in purchasing power provided by our banks during this period of bank-made inflation.

2. *Central banking coöperation.* Under the leadership of Governor Montagu Norman of the Bank of England, the heads of the leading central banks conferred on various and sundry occasions during this period. The central bankers were almost always found conspiring on the side of inflation, and they generally agreed that aggressive open market operations and lower rediscount rates were in order. The most famous of these meetings, that held in the New York Federal Reserve Bank in the summer of 1927, resulted in heavy purchases of government bonds by the Reserve Banks and a lowering of the rediscount rate—events which are generally regarded now as among the direct causes of the last spectacular phases of the stock market boom which culminated in 1929.

3. *The stock market boom,* fed by bank credit and finally by a huge expansion of "bootleg loans" made to brokers at high rates by other lenders, chiefly large corporations. The stock market went up in large measure because people were utilizing more and more bank funds to pay for stocks bought for a rise. Pools and organized manipulation ran riot during this period, but such operations were usually successful at the time only because an avid public was borrowing freely to buy shares from pool managers.

4. *A vast expansion of new issue activity.* Corporations and governments, here and abroad,

found that they could tap an almost inexhaustible stream of funds through the New York and Chicago investment bankers, with their connections all over the country. Partly as a result of bank credit expansion, partly through the great increase in national income under the stimulus of boom-time conditions, the people of this country became security buyers on an unprecedented scale. "The Commercial and Financial Chronicle," whose statistics are necessarily far from complete, reported the total volume of new financing during the decade as follows:

NEW CAPITAL ISSUES, 1920–1929

(Refunding Excluded)

Year	
1920	$ 3,634,834,192
1921	3,576,738,412
1922	4,304,362,798
1923	4,304,425,893
1924	5,593,179,972
1925	6,220,169,333
1926	6,344,133,929
1927	7,791,129,548
1928	8,114,395,681
1929	10,182,766,518

5. *Nation-wide land speculation,* similarly stimulated by bank credit expansion and the general prosperity which resulted. Banks large and small participated in the financing of real estate, aided

by the unfortunate relaxation of limitations on such loans by national banks contained in the McFadden Act of 1927. During the subsequent era of deflation, these boom-time mortgage loans on urban and agricultural real estate proved quite costly to the institutions that made them.

6. *A business boom,* which was largely spurious because based upon a persistent increase in credit that could not last. Large business corporations were fed funds by new security issues, which in turn were paid for by the buyers in large measure with borrowed funds. The expansion of brokers' loans, which attained a maximum total of some $8,000,000,000 in the fall of 1929, resulted in a direct expansion of business, for money borrowed by brokers was paid out directly to sellers of stock, to be used by them for consumption or investment purposes.

Contrary to notions widely held at the time and since, the stock market does not absorb funds. It acts merely as a channel through which borrowed funds are shifted into the hands of the sellers of securities. People who bought automobiles, homes, radios and what not during the boom period with profits made in the stock market were actually using proceeds of brokers' loans for the purpose in many instances. Excessive use of installment credit had the same evil effect.

7. *A fictitious stability of prices.* Superficial students of prices have frequently pointed to the

relative stability of the price level from 1922 to 1929 as evidence of effective control of commodity quotations. Actually, the fact that commodity prices moved within a narrow range was proof of the basic unsoundness of conditions at the time. Prices merely reflect supply and demand factors in terms of money. Widespread overproduction in many directions during this period should actually have brought about a fall in prices. This fall, which would have been a corrective to the unsound development of business at the time, was prevented, however, by the inflation of purchasing power.

8. *Continued payment of reparations and war debts with borrowed money.* Vast sums were transferred among the nations of Europe and this country during the Harding-Coolidge era of economic mismanagement. The net effect of these operations was that Germany paid the Allies large sums which the latter transferred for the most part to this country. This country then loaned to Germany and others more than enough to cover such payments. Actually, therefore, very little if anything was being paid by any one, nationally speaking, but one debt was substituted for another. As soon as borrowing could not be continued, the impossibility of paying either the old or at times the new debts in full became apparent, and the inevitable international financial collapse started.

9. *The United States proceeded to raise its*

tariff barriers to new and outlandish heights, despite the fact that it was simultaneously lending capital abroad at the rate of almost $1,500,000,000 annually. Naturally, whenever the volume of our foreign loans declined, the debtors would necessarily have to sell us more than we sold to them if they were to meet their debt service. Great Britain had found that to be the case when she gladly submitted to a so-called unfavorable balance of trade by eliminating tariff barriers in the early nineteenth century.

Herbert Hoover, first as Secretary of Commerce and later as President, stood squarely for the proposition that a great creditor nation should insist upon payment of foreign debts to it and should also raise trade barriers ever higher so as to obtain a favorable balance of trade. It will stand as a testimonial to the good sense of the average American, regardless wholly of partisan lines, that Hoover's extreme high tariff appeal in the campaign of 1932 fell upon deaf ears.

It will be noted that the above nine points all help explain the basic characteristic of the world economy of the Twenties—the creation of debt, inflation, as a weapon to combat the incipient business depression that constantly threatened the prosperity of the period. Our recent experiences clearly expose the fallacy of the fetish of Stabilization, of which many of our economists have made so much. We should learn now to welcome a reasonable amount of fluctuation instead. A moderate depression, a moderate recession in prices—these are correctives which tend to restore the economic structure to balance. When they are not permitted to take place, the economic structure, unable to purge itself of elements which make it sick, quickly develops major diseases. The day of reckoning may then be postponed, but eventually it is all the more severe and protracted by reason of the delay.

Let us turn now to a survey of the factors which made our banking structure so vulnerable to the depression which followed the inflation of the Twenties.

CHAPTER II.—WHY THE BANKS FAILED

WHAT BANK FAILURES MEAN

A BANK failure is an economic, a financial and a social disaster.

Bank failures hurt business in a number of ways. By tying up bank deposits, they reduce the supply of available purchasing power and thus contract the volume of business done. By the same token, they tend to lower commodity prices. Business men accustomed to rely upon bank loans suddenly find such customary accommodation cut off, and they are not infrequently forced to the wall as a result.

The closed bank is often liquidated, as a result of which a mass of securities and other assets are thrown on the market for sale at what they will bring. This procedure depresses prices on the exchanges. The rank and file of small depositors, finding their savings or liquid funds frozen or lost, may suffer severe personal hardship. Underlying the whole phenomenon is the undermining of confidence and security, the twin bases of capitalistic society.

So serious is the bank failure evil, that governments in a number of countries have taken drastic steps to prevent it. Only in the United States did the depression of the past few years bring in its wake a persistent and wholesale collapse of individual banks, with the serious adverse consequences outlined above.

The depression of the Thirties was not unavoidable. It was caused primarily by the great inflation of the previous decade, which had been superimposed upon an economic structure sorely in need of a period of post-war readjustment. But the depression itself would never have been as severe and as prolonged in this country as it proved to be, were it not for the very serious aggravating influence of bank failures.

A series of bank failures is very aptly called an epidemic. Failures are contagious. The collapse of one bank tends in a number of ways to hurt neighboring institutions, and if failures are numerous enough the great majority of the banks of the country may feel the effects.

The collapse of one bank of itself tends to undermine the confidence of the community and start runs on others, thus shifting the strain. Business men whose funds are tied up in one institution, if forced into bankruptcy, hurt other banks and their customers. The decline in security, real estate and other values caused by liquidation from weak and failed banks reduces the value of the assets of the remaining sound institutions.

In this way, failures of weak banks hurt the sound. Like a deadly and contagious epidemic, which strikes down healthy men and women in their prime as well as the sick and the halt, the wave of bank failures which spread over this country with unexampled and unbridled force after 1929 struck down institutions that had withstood successive panics and depressions in the past. Vast areas were left almost without banking facilities when the holocaust was over.

It should be said here that the failure of banks during the epidemic was no certain proof of weakness or mismanagement, any more than an individual who dies of yellow fever during an epidemic was necessarily unhealthy before he was struck down by the dread disease. In some parts of the country, where failures were especially numerous, individual banks were faced with the necessity at times of paying out all or nearly all of their deposits. Where this condition was faced early in the depression, before the banks had had time to prepare themselves for such an onslaught by special precautions, failure was frequently inescapable.

WHEN THE EPIDEMIC BEGAN

The post-war bank failure epidemic first assailed this country on a large scale in 1921. Collapse of land prices in the Middle West and the Northwest caused a wholesale closing down of banks in those areas. The year 1926 saw the predepression failure epidemic at its worst, as 956 institutions closed—a great many toppling with the collapse of the Florida land boom in that year. The institutions involved during this period were mainly small, local affairs, however, so that while the communities in which they were located suffered severely, the country as a whole was not affected.

Bank failures during the period from 1921 to 1929 aggregated 5,642, with total deposits of $1,721,673,000. The statistics published by the Federal Reserve Board present the following picture of failures during the great inflation period:

Bank Failures in the United States, 1921–1929

Year	*Number of Failures*	*Deposits Reported*
1921	501	$196,460,000
1922	354	110,721,000
1923	648	188,701,000
1924	776	213,338,000
1925	612	172,900,000
1926	956	272,488,000
1927	662	193,891,000
1928	491	138,642,000
1929	642	234,532,000

The record of bank failures during the decade of the Glorious Twenties, as the era was termed by the arch-inflationist among economists, Gustav Cassel, was a disgraceful chapter in the economic history of this country during the period. Even in the midst of prosperity, the American financial structure thus displayed serious structural weaknesses. While these were relatively small as compared to the number and volume of deposits of the banks that failed in the three years following the stock market panic of 1929, nevertheless the failures of the prosperity period were highly significant. They indicated that our financial structure suffered from certain basic defects which caused many individual institutions to collapse at the first onset of adversity. Obviously, something was seriously amiss, and the following years clearly proved that this was so.

A comprehensive analysis of the causes of the numerous bank failures of the thirteen year period which culminated in the banking panic of 1933 reveals three main groups of causes. These may be listed as follows:

1. Structural defects in the American banking system.
2. Managerial defects.
3. Business depression and price deflation.

BASIC DEFECTS OF AMERICAN BANKING

The major structural defect in the American banking system has been unit banking. The fear of financial concentration, of the Money Trust, had resulted in restrictions on the opening of branches by most American states and by Congress as regards national banks. Such states as Virginia authorized branch banking within its borders in the days before the Civil War, and California has been a leader in permitting state-wide branch banking since. The majority of states, however, when the failure era opened in 1921, either did not permit branch banking at all or restricted it, as did New York, New Jersey and Ohio, to city limits.

After a vigorous fight, national banks favoring branch banking were able to obtain almost the same powers in this respect as were accorded state banks in each state, through passage by Congress of the McFadden Act of 1927.

The status of branch banking in the various states, under existing laws as of May 9, 1932, summarized by the Federal Reserve Board in its July, 1932, bulletin, is given on page 27.

Opposition to branch banking has hitherto been of overwhelming strength. While based nominally upon arguments that the end of unit banking would tend to concentrate financial power in the big cities and stifle development of local communities, the real strength of the unit banking lobby, both at Washington and in the legislatures of the several states, has been deeply rooted in the narrow self-interest of many thousands of individuals and business enterprises.

FOES OF BRANCH BANKING

A list of the "natural" foes of branch banking would include:

1. Officials of unit banks, who fear loss of their posts and livelihood, or transformation of attractive positions as officers into virtual clerkships in branch banks.

2. Stockholders of unit banks, who face extinction of their equities if strong city banks should open branches in their communities and draw away deposits because of superior strength and reputation.

Summary of State Laws on Branch Banking

States permitting state-wide branch banking	*States permitting branch banking within limited areas*	*States prohibiting branch banking*	*States having no legislation regarding branch banking*
Arizona	Georgia	Alabama	Kentucky
California	Indiana	Arkansas	Michigan
Delaware	Iowa	Colorado	New Hampshire
Maryland	Louisiana	Connecticut	North Dakota
North Carolina	Maine	Florida	Oklahoma
Rhode Island	Massachusetts	Idaho	South Dakota
South Carolina	Mississippi	Illinois	Wyoming
Vermont	Montana	Kansas	
Virginia	New Jersey	Minnesota	
	New York	Missouri	
	Ohio	Nebraska	
	Pennsylvania	Nevada	
	Tennessee	New Mexico	
	Wisconsin	Oregon	
		Texas	
		Utah	
		Washington	
		West Virginia	
Total 9	Total 14	Total 18	Total 7

3. Large business corporations, especially those

whose operations cover a wide area, who prefer to keep local bankers in virtual bondage by keeping deposits with them. Certain manufacturers are able to dictate to local bankers as regards financing of their dealers and retailers in the community, etc., by leaving a substantial deposit with the local institutions and then threatening withdrawal of such deposits if their suggestions are not carried out.

4. Many of the large city banks that make large profits by acting as correspondents for interior institutions. One large metropolitan bank, reputed to have some 3,000 out-of-town correspondents, has taken the lead in opposing branch banking in every way at its command.

The American system of small unit banks represents one of the most obsolete and weakest links in our economic structure. Other leading nations, such as Great Britain, France, Germany and Canada, long ago concentrated the great bulk of their commercial banking activity into a handful of large branch banking institutions whose offices stretch across the land. Japan and Norway, two countries which had numerous unit banks until several years ago, have found it necessary to carry out a wholesale merging of their individual institutions to escape the inevitable penalty of small unit banking—bank failure epidemics in times of depression.

DEFECTS OF UNIT BANKING

Unit banking suffers from many fundamental defects. No country boasts enough talented banking management to supply several thousand individual institutions with able direction. Effective regulation and supervision of thousands of small individual banks is in practice an impossible task for the regulatory authorities. But more important than these, two fundamental weaknesses militate against safe unit banking.

In the first place, unit banking may be likened to a long chain made up of innumerable links, large and small, strong and weak. When such a chain is subjected to any material strain, some of the weak links are quite sure to break. A country with thousands of unit banks will thus find that under the strain of adverse conditions the weaker banks will topple without delay. But, as already noted, bank failures have a contagious character, so that the collapse of the weaker institutions quickly undermines the stronger.

Consider a typical community which has five banks. The assets of these institutions, in critical times, may be divided into two main groups—liquid items like bank balances and government securities which can be converted into cash within a very short time by sale or rediscounting at the Federal Reserve bank, and other assets that are frozen, although not necessarily bad. The situation may be summarized as follows:

Bank	*Per cent of Deposits Liquid*
A	10
B	20
C	30
D	40
E	50

With the onset of hard times, a withdrawal of only a small fraction of its deposits will cause Bank A to close. This of itself will stimulate the pressure of withdrawals against the other banks. Bank B, under this pressure, may be forced to close, whereupon the other banks will, more likely than not, suffer severe runs. Long lines of depositors will form at the tellers' cages to withdraw time and savings deposits, while the more effective but silent run of checking depositors drawing checks and either cashing them or depositing them in the strongest local bank, in large city banks or in savings institutions will rapidly cut down the volume of deposits of the other comparatively stronger local banks.

If all five of these banks were combined into one branch banking institution, there would be an averaging of strength and weakness. The combined institution may be only 25 per cent liquid, but these resources can be shifted to whichever branch suffers the most severe runs in the event that depositors lose confidence. As runs are met, confidence tends to be restored. Failures are avoided, and there is a correspondingly reduced need for liquidity.

Unit banking is fundamentally objectionable in the second place because it does not permit many institutions to obtain a desirable degree of diversification in their business. Small institutions in small communities become deeply involved in the specialized interests of that community. In a mining town, for example, the local institution's prosperity will tend to depend entirely upon the mining industry which it finances. If mines become depleted or employment ceases for other reasons, loans become frozen or worthless and deposits are withdrawn. The same applies to farming communities and one-industry towns in general.

SMALL CAPITALIZATION

A corollary of unit banking is the legal grant of permission for new banks to start with altogether inadequate capital resources. The National Banking Act has permitted individual banks to organize with a capital of only $25,000, in communities having less than 3,000 population, and $50,000 in communities with less than 6,000 population. In a number of states, minimum capital requirements are below those set for national banks, and in some instances they are as low as $10,000.

While the trend of American industry has been towards the evolution of giant corporate units with large liquid resources amply able to withstand hard times, obsolete banking laws, perpetuated by narrow self-interest and ill-advised popular prejudice, have artificially retained the small unit in banking. Banking is one of the most difficult of all types of business, and tends also to be one of the most speculative. A good loan will give the banker his 5 or 6 per cent in interest, a bad loan may mean the loss of the entire principal, wiping out the profits earned on a number of good investments.

The unit banking system, involving the existence of too many independent banks in individual localities, resulted in excessive and cutthroat competition. In order to attract deposits, the small banks paid high rates of interest, often well in excess of 4 per cent per annum. To earn this high rate of interest for depositors, the small banks were forced to buy bonds with high coupon rates. These were, as a rule, necessarily speculative in character. Also they made many poorly secured loans, primarily because of the attractive return which such loans offered.

The small unit banks, operating with small staffs, were not in position to select carefully the securities offered to them for sale. It is a well-known fact that bonds were sold to small banks and not bought by them. The result was that the average smaller bank held in its portfolio proportionately poorer bonds than did many larger institutions which were better equipped to handle the purchase of bonds.

The existence of a large number of small banks also led to over-lending in many cases. The relationship between the bank and its customer was frequently a personal one. Very often the officers of the bank would not or could not refuse to make loans to individuals with whom they were closely associated socially or otherwise. All these factors contributed materially to the weakness of the unit banking system.

DUAL JURISDICTION

A third structural weakness of American banking which helps explain the bank failure epidemic is the existence side by side of national and state banks, subject to 49 different laws and regulated by different authorities. During the Civil War, the National Banking System was set up by Act of Congress to provide a uniform currency backed by government bonds, as well as to help provide a market for government obligations. Under the Constitutional provision giving Congress the power to establish a uniform currency, the chartering and regulation of banks has been held to be a proper Federal function. At the same time, however, state banks have been allowed to function, although their note issues were taxed out of existence after the Civil War by an annual impost of 10 per cent on the amount outstanding.

Recent decades have witnessed keen competition between state and national jurisdictions for the chartering of banks. Many states have liberalized restrictions on banking set up in their laws in order to increase the number of institutions chartered by them. Fearful of a reduction in the number of banks subject to his control, the Comptroller of the Currency, the official who supervises national banks, has in turn begged Congress persistently to liberalize national bank laws. A situation thus arose similar to the competitive loosening of corporation laws in the various states to incease the revenues each receives from the chartering of corporations.

The organization of the Federal Reserve System in 1913, for the purpose of centralizing banking reserves and providing an elastic currency, introduced a further element of confusion. All national banks had to be members of the Federal Reserve System, while state banks might apply for membership if they met certain requirements. As a result something less than 10 per cent of all state chartered banks and trust companies have been members of the Federal Reserve System in recent years, while the great majority of the banks of the country, in number, have remained outside the system. This greatly impaired the benefits derived by the banking system as a whole from the Federal Reserve System in times of stress. The dual system of banking enables national banks to free themselves from control by the Federal Reserve System, if they desire, by changing to a state charter.

The arrival of the Great Depression thus found the American banking system altogether unprepared for the shock. On June 30, 1929, a total of 24,912 separate incorporated unit banks, of which 17,929 or 72 per cent had capital of less than $100,000, were scattered across the length and breadth of the land. Only 7,536 of these were national banks, and about one-third were members of the Federal Reserve System. Small wonder then that the failure epidemic swept over these banks like a prairie fire, leading to a steady deterioration of the banking and business structure of the country and culminating in the final collapse.

It is interesting to note that for the year ended October 31, 1932, statistics for which have been issued by the Comptroller of the Currency, fully 84.5 per cent of all bank failures occurred among institutions with capitals of less than $100,000. During the period from 1921 to October, 1932, inclusive, 1,571 national banks and 8,913 state banks failed. Of this grand total, 57.5 per cent were suspensions of banks with capitals of $25,000 or less.

BAD MANAGEMENT

Mismanagement, unwise management, inexpert management, dishonest management—American banking has suffered from all of these to a greater extent than most other economically advanced countries.

Many bankers have consistently opposed stronger banking regulation by governmental authorities on the ground that good management needs no regulation, and bad management cannot be controlled or their institutions saved by regulation. British banking, the best the world has known from many points of view, is not subject to any formal regulation or examination. But the fact of the matter is that no system has ever been devised by the ingenuity of man to provide 20,000 or 30,000 banks with good management. Experience in other countries shows that the fewer the banks, the higher the quality of banking management that is evolved.

The traditional English theory of banking is that the banker invests his deposits in a diversified list of short-term assets, chiefly loans to provide business with working capital. Such loans are expected to be self-liquidating, in that they are advanced to finance the production or sale of goods moving into consumption. As such goods are sold, funds are automatically provided for repayment of the bank loans.

American banking has from the early days of the Republic tended to depart from this sound principle. In the days of Andrew Jackson, loans on land caused a serious epidemic of wildcat bank failures which intermittently continued up to the formation of the national banking system. National banks were restricted by law to investment in liquid loans only. In course of time, however, a Comptroller of the Currency ruled that banks could buy bonds, and even before the war American bankers were showing a partiality for slower investment assets. The war stimulated this movement enormously, as banks were urged as a patriotic duty to invest in government bonds and make loans to their customers to permit the latter to do the same.

THE SHIFT TO INVESTMENT BANKING

The concentration movement in American industry, with the consequent evolution of giant corporations, profoundly affected the problems of banking management in the United States. Many of the leading industrial combinations accumulated large sums in cash from generous earnings and through the easy access they had to the capital markets through new security issues. These industrial corporations ceased to borrow from the banks, but instead became large depositors with one or more banks. Thus, when several hundred retail stores were combined into a chain, for example, the banks more often than not lost a large number of small borrowing customers, while the chain did not borrow at the banks at all, but instead kept large deposits there as free surplus cash.

The banks of the country, had they insisted upon doing liquid banking, could not have invested these deposits profitably as the number of borrowing customers declined. Interest rates would have dropped and the corporations would have been forced to buy securities for investment directly in the market to keep their surplus funds employed profitably. But most banks did not want to see their business contracted in this way. Accordingly, they turned to security investments, to security loans, to mortgages, and to other forms of investment banking to expand their portfolios. American banks ceased to a large extent to be commercial banking institutions, and became instead investment trusts. They also became interested increasingly in the business of security wholesaling and retailing, and many large metropolitan institutions formed security affiliates, stock of which was attached directly or indirectly to stock of the bank, which could engage in business forbidden to the bank but could borrow funds from the bank to finance such prohibited operations.

These conditions put a premium on bad banking management, unavoidable as much of that was in any event under a unit banking system. They left our banking structure standing like a house of cards when the wave of depression and deflation came along after 1929.

The structural weaknesses, the deficiencies in management of American banking, traced above, explain the sad record established by it through three years of depression. The test of strength of a banking system is had, not during a period of prosperity when rising values tend to cover over mistakes, but rather during a depression. As business volume declines and commodity prices drop, profits dwindle or are wiped out altogether. As a result, many loans become "slow, doubtful or bad," the three qualities of deterioration recognized by bank examiners. Security and real estate values drop, undermining the quality of collateral loans as well as the investments of the banks.

At such a time, a strong banking structure and good banking management manifest themselves most effectively. The Canadian banks, the English banks, withstood the onslaught of depression and withstood it well. Our banking system, we learned to our sorrow, displayed no similar sturdy qualities.

In the next chapter, we shall trace whatever efforts were made to correct the basic banking abuses during the early stages of the depression and the great bank failure epidemic which marked it.

CHAPTER III.—EFFORTS AT REFORM—THE GLASS BILL

APATHY OF CONGRESS

A NATION, faced with major disaster, usually seeks to ward off the threatened evil by governmental action. When Democracy becomes so inefficient that it cannot protect itself against catastrophe, it often gives way to dictatorship of one kind or another.

The bank failure epidemic was a significant test of the efficacy of Democracy in the United States. It raged with special force for the greater part of three years, however, before a change in Administration and a nation-wide bank holiday brought home to legislature and people at least the realization of the need for basic reform.

This should not be taken to imply that no efforts at reform were made earlier. Banking has long been a highly regulated industry as conducted in the United States, in sharp contrast to England. Regulation had been utilized, however, to quote a leading British critic of American finance, Dr. T. E. Gregory, "to impose permanently on the country a banking system appropriate to the conditions of 1860, under the combined influence of the doctrine of 'State rights' and local small-town patriotism." But American banking has not lacked able critics at home, and several of these were in position to force the situation on the attention of Congress. The latter, however, adopted only half-hearted measures or passed some ineffective emergency legislation.

The most important banking legislation passed in the decade of the Twenties was the McFadden-Pepper bill of 1927. This measure, however, in no sense constituted a reform. It sought rather specifically to legalize and extend the "new era" practices of the day. It gave statutory authorization to banks to buy virtually any corporate bonds, it extended greatly their authority to buy real estate mortgages, and it permitted banks to split up their stocks into shares of less than $100 par value.

The banking investigations conducted by the Banking and Currency Committees of the House of Representatives and of the Senate before 1931 proved to be mainly opportunities for a number of bankers to come down to Washington to explain and eulogize their practices for the benefit of unsophisticated and often overawed members of the national legislature. There were, however, a few who clearly saw the defects of the American banking system and who suggested drastic changes.

The collapse of the Bank of United States at the end of 1930, the result primarily of the use of half the bank's capital funds to purchase its own stock, was in many respects the largest bank failure in the history of the world to that date. It precipitated a new panic, but of much smaller proportions than in 1929, in the nation's money center. It dramatically centered the attention of the country for a time on the bank failure problem. This failure of an institution with some $200,000,000 of deposits belonging to 400,000 individual depositors in 60 branch offices throughout the metropolis made millions everywhere question the solvency of their own banks for the first time.

That the Bank of United States' collapse brought about an intensification of the bank failure epidemic may be seen from statistics of bank failures before and after its closing early in December, 1930.

BANK FAILURES BY MONTHS

1930	*Number*	*Deposits*
September	66	$ 23,666,000
October	72	24,599,000
November	254	186,306,000
December	344	367,119,000
1931		
January	202	78,130,000
February	77	35,123,000
March	86	35,285,000

The House Committee on Banking and Currency was headed by Representative Louis T. McFadden of Pennsylvania, himself a country banker and the author of the 1927 McFadden bill. This committee held a series of hearings, beginning with February, 1931, and extending through the year, into branch, chain and group banking. Although many opinions were heard and a mass of facts elicited, no results were achieved.

THE SENATE INVESTIGATES

The Senate Banking and Currency Committee was headed, during the Hoover Administration, by Senator Peter Norbeck of So. Dakota. Generally classified as a western Progressive, Norbeck was considerably less radical than most members of the Upper House included in this bloc. He had but slight technical knowledge of banking, and both by tradition and affiliation he was antipathetic to branch banking. Senator Norbeck fully realized his own limitations, however. Aroused by the bank failures of the period to the need for a thorough banking investigation, he appointed Carter Glass, veteran Democrat and author of the Federal Reserve Act, to the post of chairman of a sub-committee of five to carry on the probe. The Glass sub-committee, with H. Parker Willis as chief technical adviser, launched a survey of the banking situation through questionnaire investigations and public hearings which lasted through the early months of 1931.

Many of the major factors surrounding the bank failure epidemic discussed above were brought out in the hearings of the Glass sub-committee and in its reports based on questionnaire studies. Weaknesses of unit banks, existence of frozen assets through resort by the banks to investment operations, the abuses inherent in the system of security affiliates—these can all be found described in the volumes published by the committee. The investigation was conducted, however, with a studied attempt to avoid the spectacular and the personal. Evidence of personal wrong-doing or items reflecting on the standing of particular solvent institutions were not given publicity.

A southern gentleman to the core, Senator Glass sought to get at the heart of the banking problem as such, instead of transforming himself into a criminal prosecutor. Events proved, however, that the method he followed was not calculated to bring results at that time. The later investigation by Ferdinand Pecora in 1933, which went over some of the same operations but concentrated on personal wrong-doings of individuals in high financial places, proved far more effective in crystallizing public sentiment in favor of sweeping banking reform.

WHY BANKERS FOUGHT REFORM

The Glass investigation brought out in clear relief the fact that the rank and file of bankers of the country, while quite willing to come down to Washington to testify about their business and the state of the country in general (not a single subpœna was used by Senator Glass to force the attendance of witnesses), did not want any legislation passed. In fact, the opposition of bankers was to a considerable extent responsible for the failure of the Hoover Administration to pass a single permanent constructive banking measure despite the bank failure epidemic that raged through most of its term of office. Palliatives, "psychological poultices" in the words of Carter Glass, were passed in profusion. The basic banking law of the country remained unchanged.

There is a tradition in Canada that the banking law ought to be brought up to date about once in ten years, with bankers doing the job of modernization. This is as it should be. In the United States, however, there has been a startling lack of coöperation on the part of the bankers themselves in the evolution of banking legislation. Loud in their complaints against inexpert and demagogic legislation, and rightly so, they nevertheless made no move to make legislation by the demagogue unnecessary by suggesting effective legislation themselves. It is a matter of record that the Federal Reserve Act was almost forced down the throats of the New York bankers by a relatively unfriendly Wilson administration. An even more bitter opposition was to be met by Carter Glass when he introduced a banking law based on the findings of his investigations.

Three main reasons may be advanced for the extreme distaste displayed by bankers towards new legislation affecting their business, no matter how serious the abuses that cry for reform.

First, there is the inherent conservatism of the American banker. He is afraid of any change in the law which might disturb the existing situation, no matter how unsatisfactory that situation may be. Living in a highly hazardous and uncertain world as one of many thousands of unit banks in a highly fluctuating economy, he prefers any certainty to the uncertainty of legislative change. The more conservative the banker, often, the greater his fear of legislation which might weaken what he regards as his own particular impregnable position. Many a conservative banker regards as the sum total of his responsibilities in adverse times the assurance that his bank can open the next day and meet any demands on it in sight. The more difficult mental processes involved in seeking at the same time to influence a reorganization of a whole banking system he instinctively avoids.

In the second place, opposition to reform arises from the small unit bankers all over the country who fear branch banking above all else. Bankers from the forks of the creeks bring steady pressure to bear upon their representatives and senators to fight anything and everything which would impair their position by liberalizing branch banking powers of the larger and stronger city banks, or otherwise impair their position of splendid isolation.

A third major source of opposition to banking reform is the individual and the institution that has benefited from practices which the proposed reform would curb or eliminate. Thus, when Senator Glass proposed to do away with security affiliates, in view of the fact that these latter institutions permitted the management of a bank to engage in any and every type of business under the sun, if they wished, with the use of money borrowed from the banks themselves, powerful organized opposition was offered by officials of security-affiliates, and banks whose affairs were so closely intertwined with their affiliates that they shuddered at the thought of separation. Some of the officials of the more conservative security affiliates suggested government supervision instead of segregation to eliminate abuses, but even on this there was no unanimity.

The bankers of the United States, taken as a whole, have been consistent opponents of any basic changes in banking laws. Individual bankers and groups of bankers have favored specific legislation needed to facilitate their own business. The banking community may come solidly to favor emergency legislation to prevent a crisis. But a reasoned attempt to recognize and correct obvious evils by legislation in normal times usually meets a powerful wall of opposition.

Furthermore, this opposition can be remarkably effective. Bankers as a group exercise a powerful influence over Congress and the Administration. This is due partly to the leading position of bankers in their communities. It is due also to the glamour and prestige the banker possesses in the eyes of politicians. The Federal Reserve Act of 1913 would have been, in all probability, a far different measure if continuous efforts were not made before its passage to temper its provisions so as to obtain at least negative support from banking groups. Senator Glass' new banking bill similarly was changed continuously throughout its legislative career of almost two years, in an endeavor to make its passage possible in the face of banking opposition.

THE FEDERAL RESERVE AND REFORM

The Federal Reserve System constitutes the central bank of the United States. In order to avoid the centralization associated with central banks generally, however, the framers of the Federal Reserve Act established 12 regional banks and a supervisory Federal Reserve Board in Washington in place of a single institution. Leadership in efforts to reform the banking situation so as to stem the tide of bank failures would naturally be expected from the Federal Reserve Board.

When the bank failure epidemic began, the Federal Reserve Board was headed by Roy A. Young, a northwestern banker who stood in much awe of big city bankers and displayed a notable lack of leadership. President Hoover, disturbed by the collapse of the banking structure under his very eyes, resorted to a "shake-up" of the Federal Reserve Board early in 1931. Mr. Young had his salary stepped up from $12,000 to $25,000 a year by being shifted to the post of Governor of the Federal Reserve Bank of Boston. Edmund H. Platt, vice-governor of the board, resigned to accept an executive post with a group banking organization in New York State. This left the way to the appointment of a New Yorker as governor, and Eugene Meyer, Jr., once head of the War Finance Corporation and the man who had warned Hoover consistently that the banking situation needed correction, was inducted into the post.

Governor Meyer is best known in recent years for his efforts to check the great bank failure conflagration by temporary expedients such as the Reconstruction Finance Corporation. He was also keenly interested in permanent reform of banking through legislation, however.

It was a characteristic of the Hoover régime that problems were tackled through the expedient of forming commissions to study them. When in doubt, Mr. Hoover called a conference or appointed a commission. Eugene Meyer showed a similar predilection. Two committees of the Federal Reserve System, including officials of several Reserve Banks and the Reserve Board, were appointed to study the problem of branch, chain and group banking and to analyze the problem of bank reserves.

The committee on branch, chain and group banking, after extensive researches, prepared a report said to favor a marked extension of branch banking as a means of checking bank failures. This report has not been made public to date, an indication once again of the powerful and organized vested interests which stand opposed to branch banking.

The committee on reserves issued a relatively innocuous proposal that banking reserves be calculated on the basis of the velocity of turnover of banking deposits, rather than their amount. Ingenious from the theoretical standpoint, this plan was open to a variety of practical objections, and appears consigned to limbo.

Governor Meyer's contribution to banking legislation was not a glorious one. He displayed a distinct inability to coöperate with Congressional committees. The same domineering personal qualities which made his chief a failure in the White House were possessed by Meyer to a considerable degree. His most constructive proposal was one to end state banks and make all commercial banking institutions take out national charters, but he failed to push the suggestion vigorously.

The Comptroller of the Currency, the guardian and superintendent of the national banking system, has in the past frequently recommended new banking legislation. Comptroller John W. Pole's chief contribution to discussion of banking reform was his advocacy of "trade area" branch banking. Mr. Pole was never very specific about what trade areas were, indicating that they would constitute the regions around important cities, and his influence on new legislation was nil.

The Chamber of Commerce of the United States also launched an inquiry into the banking system, and sent out a questionnaire to its members to formulate a policy on banking reform. The program, when presented, included a number of minor suggestions for changes in banking laws and regulations, and failed to take a decisive attitude towards the more fundamental issues.

It is evident that the bank failure epidemic uncovered a notable lack of constructive leadership. The Hoover Administration, the Federal Reserve Board, the banking community and the Comptroller of the Currency either opposed or adopted a passive rôle towards the subject of a really comprehensive banking reform, while a number of makeshifts such as the Reconstruction Finance Corporation, the Glass-Steagall Bill and similar efforts to stall off the day of reckoning were enacted into law.

E

THE GLASS BANKING BILL

Only the Banking and Currency Committee of the United States Senate concerned itself with the problem of fundamental banking reform, through the investigation launched by its sub-committee headed by Carter Glass.

The hearings of the Glass sub-committee culminated in the introduction in the Senate of the Glass banking reform bill on January 21, 1932. This measure consisted of a number of amendments to the National Banking Act and the Federal Reserve Act. Its chief provisions were:

1. The Federal Reserve System was authorized specifically to control bank credit so as to prevent expansion of security loans. A number of detailed provisions were included to permit curtailment or suspensions of privileges to banks that increased their security loans despite warnings against so doing by the Federal Reserve Board.

2. The commercial banks were to be taken out of investment banking as far as feasible through segregation of security affiliates from parent institutions, elimination of investment bankers from the boards of directors of commercial banks and restrictions on underwriting and other security buying and selling activities by the banks. Their real estate activities were curtailed also.

3. Banks were to be prohibited from making loans to brokers for the account of their custom-

ers, the so-called "brokers' loans for the account of others" which made credit control by the Reserve banks more difficult during the security market boom period.

4. A Federal Liquidating Corporation was set up, to facilitate the liquidation of failed banks and hasten distributions of the assets held in the form of payments to their depositors.

5. State-wide branch banking was provided.

The introduction of the Glass Bill was the signal for one of the most violent and vociferous attacks delivered against any measure brought before Congress witnessed in years. Bankers' associations, individual financiers and chambers of commerce joined in condemning it as a vicious bill and an insuperable bar to economic recovery. Even many of those who sympathized with its objectives argued that the time was not propitious for bank reform, an inevitable argument which results in most vital banking legislation being accomplished only under the pressure of panic or crisis.

Faced with this barrage of opposition, the sponsors of the Glass Bill proceeded to tone it down in the hope of obtaining its passage. Opposition was particularly strong from two quarters—many leading New York bankers who sought to save their security affiliates, and unit bankers who opposed the branch banking provisions. Despite such emasculation of the measure, however, it could not pass Congress. Finally, in greatly mutilated form, it did ultimately pass the Senate in the closing days of the Hoover administration, after Senator Huey Long of Louisiana had carried on an extensive filibuster, on the very eve of the banking panic, to stop its passage. Senator Long thus became, ironically enough, the ally of the New York bankers who were still waging their forlorn fight to save their affiliates, a fight abandoned shortly thereafter when intensive popular indignation was aroused by the disclosures concerning the management of the National City Bank and its security affiliate under Charles E. Mitchell's management. The termination of organized banking opposition to the measure was clearly indicated in the famous Aldrich statement, in which President Winthrop W. Aldrich of the Chase National Bank himself condemned the practices of its security affiliate and promised its early segregation.

THE A. B. A. IS SILENT

The reception accorded the Glass Bill definitely revealed that the bankers of the country did not care to reform the banking situation themselves. The convention of the American Bankers Association in Los Angeles, in October, 1932, only five months before the bank panic, brought out in high relief the fact that, however much individual bankers and groups of bankers labored and struggled to fight the failure epidemic, the banking profession as such was wholly unable to unite on a program.

The American Bankers Association has long proved inconsequential in many respects, owing to the predominance of small unit bankers among its membership. It has studiously avoided controversial banking issues. At the 1932 convention, it actually refrained from taking any position at all on branch banking. Under the circumstances, it is not at all surprising that most of those attending concentrated their attention upon such issues as fees to be charged for trust service and small checking accounts, or shifted their interest away from banking to the golf course.

Nero, tradition says, fiddled while Rome burned. The American bankers played golf and talked much nonsense in October, 1932, while the bank failure epidemic was raging all over the country. Among the choice morsels contained in the news reports of the convention are these—

"The unit bankers organized a special group to fight branch banking. Speeches before this group indicated that only rogues or knaves favored banking concentration. . . .

"President Henry J. Haas, in his presidential address, told the assembled bankers of the nation that no class of business or business men in the nation to-day represents more capable management, sounder financial conditions and a greater capacity for public service than do the present

19,500 institutions that make up our banking structure. . . .

"Mr. Haas pointed out that people exaggerated the significance of the 2,300 bank failures during the year 1931, by talking about the $1,690,000,000 in deposits of these banks as if they were all lost. Depositors in such banks received some of their money back in liquidating dividends. . . ."

Mr. Haas apparently regarded these dividends as charitable donations to depositors from the "capable managements" of the failed banks. The President of the A. B. A. described the constructive attitude of the association towards efforts at banking reform by saying: "Bankers are not always in opposition to important measures affecting banking. All they ask is that these measures be sound, timely and in the real public interest."

It required a major national catastrophe to change the attitude of the banking community towards the subject of banking legislation, and to bring home to them the inevitability of changes in our organic banking law. In the meanwhile, events in Europe were helping to precipitate this final crisis, and we shall turn to a survey of them in the two following chapters.

CHAPTER IV.—THE PRELUDE IN EUROPE

RUMBLINGS OF DISASTER

In 1930, the stage was set for one of the world's greatest financial upheavals in history. The flimsy international financial structure built up after the war with the aid of American capital functioned well enough in the halcyon days of inflation, but with the first onslaught of the economic depression its inherent weakness was revealed. The collapse of the speculative boom in the United States, the sudden cessation of the international movement of capital, and the inability of the European statesmen to face economic realities evidenced in the negotiations concerning the Young Plan were severe shocks which rocked the international financial machinery to its very foundation.

The German elections of September, 1930, indicated clearly the revolt of the German masses against the Treaty of Versailles and the burden of reparations. It revealed unmistakably the revival of a spirit of militant nationalism. The changed political attitude of the German nation thus added political to economic uncertainties. The international money market became highly nervous. Lenders became cautious about their

European commitments, while the more far-sighted financiers in the United States and France began slowly to withdraw their short-term loans from Central Europe. The entire post-war financial structure, built up like a house of cards, awaited only a minor storm to blow it over.

THE AUSTRIAN COLLAPSE

It was in Austria, a country so crippled by the Treaty of Peace that it had to be sustained throughout the post-war period by large and continuous foreign loans, that the storm began. The origin of the Austrian financial crisis is to be found in one of those conflicts between political policy and economic necessity which have characterized post-war Europe. Without taking adequate preliminary diplomatic steps, Germany and Austria on March 20, 1931, suddenly announced to the world that a customs union between the two countries was being negotiated. This notice of impending economic union brought forth vigorous protests from the Little Entente, France's political allies, and aroused great resentment in France. The French, at the height of their financial hegemony, immediately began to utilize their financial power to prevent the projected economic union between the two German speaking peoples. They little realized that the breaking of the financial backbone of Austria would set in motion forces comparable in magnitude to those resulting from the shot of the assassin at Sarajevo, which covered Europe with blood and destruction for years.

Suddenly, and like a bolt from the sky, the financial centers of the world were shocked by the revelation on May 11, 1931, that the Austrian Credit Anstalt, the largest and most respected banking institution in Austria, had applied to the Austrian government and to the Austrian National Bank for assistance. Withdrawals of French deposits were blamed by many at the time as the immediate cause of the difficulties. The difficulties of the Austrian Credit Anstalt, a Rothschild institution of which Louis Rothschild, a senior partner of the Vienna house, was Chairman of the Board, revealed in a glaring light the economic and political instability of the post-war era. The fall of this one institution precipitated a series of financial crises which reached a climax only with the closing of the New York banks on March 4, 1933.

The Credit Anstalt represented economic Austria. It controlled nearly two-thirds of the industrial production of Austria, and its resources amounted to 70 per cent of the total assets of all the banks of the country. Its excellent reputation and extensive foreign connections had enabled it to borrow relatively large amounts of short-term funds, which it used to maintain and even to increase its commitments at home and in the Succession States of the old Austro-Hungarian Empire. Thus, its collapse had widespread ramifications and its financial difficulties affected not only the entire Austrian economic and financial structure, but involved a number of institutions in other countries as well.

Realizing the seriousness of the situation, the Austrian government used every means at its disposal to bolster up the tottering Credit Anstalt. Nevertheless, foreign withdrawals continued and a domestic run developed, with frantic depositors throughout Austria besieging the windows of this old institution, clamoring for what was left of their pre-war fortunes. Finally, the government, by law of May 28, 1931, guaranteed all foreign liabilities of the Credit Anstalt and, on June 26, 1931, the guarantee was extended to cover domestic liabilities.

The second phase of the Austrian crisis, in which French finance played a leading rôle, involved Austrian efforts to obtain foreign financial aid. The huge withdrawal of foreign funds so seriously depleted the reserves of the Austrian National Bank that it applied for and promptly obtained a credit of 100,000,000 schillings ($14,070,000) from the Bank for International Settlements and a group of central banks, including the Bank of France and the Federal Reserve Banks. However, this temporary aid was not sufficient. The blow was so severe that further assistance was needed and this assistance could come only from abroad. The Austrian government applied to the League of Nations Commission on Austrian Control for permission to contract a foreign loan of about $21,000,000 and this permission was granted. It was proposed to place this loan in Paris, Berlin, London and New York. The old European plague of politics interfered again, however, and France made its participation contingent upon the fulfilment of certain political conditions. It demanded the renunciation of the customs-union with Germany as the price of its participation in a loan of which France's share was to be not more than approximately $11,000,000. Austria was either unwilling or unable to meet this political demand and the Bank of England, the traditional stabilizer of international finance, advanced the entire amount from its own resources.

This action of the Bank of England, however, proved quite costly to Great Britain. It aroused the ire of the French, who held huge balances in England, and who knew only too well the great danger in which Great Britain would find herself if these balances were withdrawn.

Here, too, the lack of foresight as well as the selfishness of individuals and nations manifested itself. The statesmen of Europe, instead of visualizing the impending collapse and of buttressing the weakest point in the financial structure of

Europe, allowed petty animosities and political intrigues to have their way, thereby accelerating the climax of the drama which was soon to come.

The collapse of the Credit Anstalt destroyed almost with one stroke the widely heralded achievements in financial reconstruction of the League of Nations. Its effects were immediately felt in all neighboring countries. Banks in a number of South Eastern European countries began to close their doors, and before long the rumblings of the earthquake began to be heard in Germany.

GERMANY IS AFFECTED

The economic reconstruction of Germany was financed with money borrowed abroad. More than two billion dollars were obtained by long-term bond issues, and another billion and a half were borrowed in the form of short-term loans and credits. These latter short-term foreign obligations particularly constituted the Achilles heel in the German national economy. This weakness was not unknown to France, and more than once the latter utilized financial weapons to bring Germany to terms. True, the Armistice of November 11, 1918, brought to a halt the utilization of destructive war weapons, but the war continued, none the less, although fought with financial weapons.

In 1929 and in 1930 the French turned their heavy financial guns on the German national economy and, through the withdrawal of funds directly or indirectly, shook the foundations of the German national economy. Germany was ill-prepared for a new financial onslaught. Her economic power was weakened by the war, by the treaties of peace and by the ravages of an unprecedented currency inflation. Since the initial Hitler electoral victory in September, 1930, she had been subject to a slow but continuous withdrawal and cancellation of foreign short-term credits.

The collapse of the Credit Anstalt started an external run on German debtors, banks and corporations alike, which up to that time was practically unprecedented in modern history. During the first seven months of 1931, withdrawals of foreign credits and flight of capital deprived Germany of approximately 3,500,000,000 marks. This huge transfer of funds greatly decreased the liquidity of the great German banks and, above all, it put the stability of the German mark in jeopardy. Determined to prevent depreciation of the currency, the Reichsbank sold hundreds of millions of dollars of gold and foreign exchange to support the mark on the markets of the world, thereby seriously depleting its metallic reserves. This situation forced the Reichsbank to apply for foreign financial assistance and, on June 25, 1931, the

Bank for International Settlements, the Bank of England, the Bank of France and the Federal Reserve Bank of New York granted a short-term credit of $100,000,000. Shortly thereafter the Gold Discount Bank, a subsidiary of the Reichsbank, availed itself of a $50,000,000 credit previously established with a syndicate of American banks.

Such aid, however, was a mere drop in the bucket. It soon became evident that immediate relief of major character was necessary to prevent Germany from following Austria in financial collapse. The British government, fully aware of the gravity of the situation, supported the German efforts to obtain further financial assistance from abroad, but the efforts of the German government were in vain and a collapse seemed unavoidable. Suddenly and without warning President Hoover made his historic proposal for a one-year moratorium on reparations and war debts. A miracle had happened. There was an immediate change in the psychology and sentiment of the people throughout the world. Prices of commodities and securities throughout the world began to rise and for the moment it looked as if the crisis had been overcome and that a new era of good will and international coöperation had begun.

The optimists, however, made their calculations without considering France. Up to that time France had felt only slightly the severe economic depression prevailing throughout the world. With the exception of a few political loans to its Allies, France did not engage in long-term foreign lending on a large scale, but preferred to keep her financial ammunition in the form of gold and short-term investments accumulated in huge amounts in the London and New York money markets. This ammunition was a powerful weapon in the hands of France, because her financiers and political leaders were fully aware of the disastrous effects of any sudden withdrawal of these funds, particularly from London.

France saw in the Hoover moratorium not only an important loss of revenue which would result in increased burdens on her own taxpayers, but also an end of the recently signed Young Plan and the first step in the direction of revising the political status of Europe as established by the peace treaties. France, however, was firmly determined to maintain the *status quo,* not only politically but also financially, and saw in the European financial crisis an opportunity to establish a lasting financial hegemony over Europe. The bickering by France and the insistence on legal technicalities consumed precious time, and when, on July 6, two weeks after the Hoover proposal was made, an agreement between the United States and France was reached, it was already too late.

THE GERMAN BANKS CLOSE

Confidence failed to revive, the external run on

Germany continued undiminished, a flight of capital from Germany set in and German citizens began to withdraw their bank deposits. The failure of a large corporation in Germany in which the Darmstaedter und National (Danat) Bank was financially involved further impaired public confidence in this important Berlin bank, and it became obvious that without assistance from the government or from the other large German banks, the Danat Bank would have to close its doors. The large German banks, instead of acting in unison for their common welfare, engaged in pin pricking politics motivated by selfish purposes and personal animosity against some of the officials of the Danat Bank. Little did they realize that the closing of one large bank would create a furor on the part of the depositors which none of them could withstand. The officials of each bank considered only their own position and failed to realize that the banking system of no country can convert the mass of its deposits into cash on short notice.

On July 13, 1931, the Danat Bank was closed, and its closing was followed immediately by a general run on all German banks. There was nothing left but for all banks to close their doors for a time. It is remarkable how the banking crisis in Germany in 1931 resembled conditions in the United States in 1933. One merely has to change names from Berlin to Detroit and from Germany to the United States to see the close similarity between the two situations. This, however, merely proves the truth of the old saying that one seldom learns from the experience of others.

The temporary closing of the whole banking system of the country was the first in the history of modern German banking. Such a drastic step was not taken even during the desperately chaotic monetary conditions of 1922 and 1923. Although the German government took prompt action to reopen the banks and to effect a thorough reorganization of banking in Germany, the closing of the German banks had a fatal effect on confidence in other countries. The financial panic spread like wild fire, and created a general demand by nations and institutions for their deposits or their short-term credits held abroad.

THE RUN ON LONDON

This panicky liquidation of foreign short-term credits was bound to have a disastrous effect on London, the financial center of the world. When the financial crisis broke out in Central Europe, London, true to its tradition as a great international money center, did all in its power to prevent the spread of the conflagration and to bring order out of chaos. The Bank of England had extended a credit of $21,000,000 to Austria in opposition to France, whose financial institutions were the

F

chief creditors on the London money market, and it had participated to the extent of $25,000,000 in a credit granted to the German Reichsbank. In addition, London was forced to render financial assistance to various members of the far-flung British Empire in order to enable them to meet their obligations falling due in London and in New York. These steps were taken by England at a time when the London money market was a debtor on a large scale, and when it was well known that its commitments in Central Europe and in a number of South American countries were solidly frozen.

The French, aroused by the loan granted by the Bank of England to Austria, began to withdraw their funds from the London market. This was followed by withdrawals by other countries. During the months of July and August, London lost approximately 200,000,000 pounds or about $1,000,000,000. The gold holdings of the Bank of England dwindled rapidly, its discount rate was raised from 2½ per cent to 3½ per cent, and finally on July 30 to 4½ per cent. The report of the Parliament's Economy Committee (May Committee), which revealed the difficulties of the British Budget, further undermined confidence in the London market and accelerated withdrawals of funds from abroad.

The Bank of France had huge balances in England, estimated at the time at about 60,000,000 pounds or $292,000,000 and immediately realized that the suspension of gold payments by the Bank of England would mean a tremendous loss. It began to support the pound, but this support came too late.

Great Britain was fighting a desperate battle. In spite of the views which prevailed later that the abandonment of specie payments was beneficial for Great Britain, the Bank of England and the British Treasury resorted to every means at their command to maintain the gold standard. On August 1, the Bank of England obtained foreign credits of $250,000,000, half from the Federal Reserve Bank of New York and half from the Bank of France. These loans, however, were inadequate to allay the fears of creditors and to restore confidence. By the end of August, the $250,000,000 of foreign credits had been used up, the Bank of England found itself in a still weaker position, and the rush of withdrawals continued. But England did not give up the fight. On August 28, the British Treasury concluded arrangements to borrow $200,000,000 from an American financial group, and to obtain another $200,000,000 through a French banking syndicate. These loans were contracted on terms which in the pre-war period would have been demanded only of a South American country or of China. Britain swallowed her pride to remain solvent and maintain the stability of her currency.

ENGLAND ABANDONS GOLD

But the avalanche of foreign withdrawals, once set in motion, could not be stopped. It went on with irresistible force and, when no more foreign assistance even on onerous terms was forthcoming, Great Britain for the second time in 134 years was forced to suspend specie payments.

On September 20, the Cabinet ratified the resolution to suspend the gold standard provisionally for a period of six months, and on September 21, 1931, the London money market, that great bulwark of strength, financial tradition and conservatism, was forced to declare itself unable to pay its foreign creditors in full. The discount rate of the Bank of England was raised to 6%, a rate uncommon in peace time; the Stock Exchange was closed; but the British nation kept its nerve. It is a high tribute indeed to British depositors, to their sense of patriotism, that they retained their poise and did not start runs on the banks. It revealed in dramatic fashion the confidence and trust of the British in their financial institutions, which contrasted sharply with the attitude of the people in the United States.

In spite of the fact that many leading financiers in Great Britain and in the United States acclaimed the abandonment of the gold standard by Great Britain as a favorable development, it was in many respects a calamity of the first magnitude. It spelled the end of the entire post-war program of financial rehabilitation of Europe. It destroyed the last vestige of international financial confidence and brought to an end the period of currency stabilization accomplished with such great efforts only a few years before. It meant the end of the gold exchange standard, which had been heralded as a new and modern invention to make gold work overtime, and finally, it meant the complete breakdown of the gold standard itself.

Great Britain fought the battle with all the weapons at her disposal. She formed a coalition government. She was the only great world power to take decisive steps to balance her budget and she even contracted debts abroad at terms which only six months before would have been considered as usurious and unbelievable. She borrowed from the United States, a country which she had assisted with her own capital in the transition from economic infancy to maturity. She borrowed from France, a country which had asked and obtained from Great Britain a remission of a substantial part of her war debt. England, who since 1925 had led and helped other nations to return to the gold standard, was the first to abandon it. The pound sterling had fallen, in the words of a great French economist and financier, Charles Rist, "like a good soldier, fighting for the stability of the European currencies."

The abandonment of specie payments by Great Britain was followed by similar action in a number of countries. The Scandinavian countries, whose economic life is closely tied up with that of Great Britain, immediately followed suit and suspended gold payments. Practically all the British Dominions and colonies with the exception of South Africa followed the example set by Great Britain and promptly abandoned the gold standard. South Africa clung to the gold standard until the end of 1932, when even this greatest gold producing country in the world was forced to abandon gold conversion of her currency. A number of other countries, such as Austria, Germany and Hungary, which because of internal conditions could not afford to let their currencies depreciate, adopted rigid foreign exchange restrictions, prohibited the exportation of capital and established strict governmental supervision of all international financial transactions. By the end of 1932, with the exception of the United States, France, Holland, Switzerland, Belgium and Poland, every country in the world had either definitely abandoned the gold standard or had adopted such rigid foreign exchange restrictions that they had in practice given up the international gold standard as that term was previously understood.

EFFECTS OF COLLAPSE OF THE POUND

The abandonment of specie payments by Great Britain, most of the British Dominions and Colonies, the Scandinavian countries, Japan and others dethroned gold from the dominant position it had held as a basis for currency and credit. No longer did the central banks of these and other countries pay any attention to the proportion or ratio of their gold holdings to the volume of bank notes or deposits outstanding. The gold standard, hitherto upheld by many as the only possible standard under the modern economic system, was suddenly subject to attack as being the chief cause of the depression. The financial soothsayers who for years had been predicting that the world was about to be confronted with a shortage of gold, let out a howl of "I told you so." But what had happened revealed no fundamental defect of the gold standard—no shortage of the precious metal. The gold standard broke down only because of the insane economic and political policies established after the war. The very fact that the gold standard did break down under such circumstances was proof of its soundness as a governor of the economic mechanism. The gold standard was held to be dead, and hardly had it breathed its last when the cohorts rallied around the new kings, Managed Currency and Controlled Inflation, whose adherents multiplied enormously almost over night.

THE ERA OF DEFAULTS

By this time the collapse of the international money market was complete. In each country, there was a frantic rush to withdraw funds from wherever those funds could still be withdrawn. A new banking terminology developed, hitherto unknown and unheard of. Standstill agreements, providing for the freezing of short-term foreign credits, were concluded between debtors in Austria, Germany and Hungary and their foreign creditors. Trading in a new type of foreign exchange, "blocked accounts," arose and gave ample opportunities for those speculators who love to fish in troubled waters and perform needed economic functions while obtaining advantages for themselves from the misery of others.

Defaults and international bankruptcies on a large scale set in. At the beginning of 1931, only a few foreign loans floated in the post-war period were in default, but during 1931 and 1932 foreign government defaults became general. The finances of countries like Chile, which for decades had promptly met principal and interest on their external obligations, collapsed completely. Most of the South American governments, states, provinces and municipalities defaulted on their external debts in rapid succession. In Europe, nation after nation declared its inability to pay. Austria, Hungary, Yugoslavia, Bulgaria and Greece suspended payments, some of them even on loans contracted under the auspices of the League of Nations. The great prestige which the League had built up in executing its program of post-war financial reconstruction was suddenly destroyed, and at the end of 1931 the world found itself in an economic quagmire greater even than in the years immediately following the war.

The significance of the League's loss of financial prestige did not become apparent immediately. It will only be realized fully when economic reconstruction begins anew. In the future, the fact that a loan is being issued under the auspices of the League will no longer be an inducement to trusting investors to buy bonds of economically weak countries. Without the influence of the League, the future reconstruction of Europe will be a much more complicated and difficult task. The collapse of 1931–32 and the defaults on League of Nations loans thereby not only brought to a halt the reconstruction activities of the League of Nations, but it made very difficult if not impossible its future financial assistance.

The collapse of the pound, the abandonment of the gold standard by a number of countries, the wholesale rejection of the gold exchange standard and, above all, the liquidation of short-term foreign balances wherever possible have greatly diminished the amount of credit and capital available for the financing of international transactions. High tariffs, import quotas and foreign exchange restrictions have reduced international trade to a lower level than at any time in the last twenty-five years or longer. The economic depression brought a degree of suffering and hardship to people in many countries equal to and even greater than that caused by the World War. Unemployment increased rapidly everywhere, and disaster engulfed all countries without exception. Prices of commodities, raw materials as well as manufactured goods, continued their inevitable downward march as markets were contracted or destroyed, and were followed by a further decline in security prices, particularly in the United States.

The economic depression in this country became especially acute and one of its manifestations was large deficits in the budget of the Federal government. The foreign banking institutions which still held balances in New York in large amounts began to look with fear and dismay on this development and on the growing demand for inflation and currency depreciation within this country. The collapse of the pound sterling undermined their confidence in the stability of even the strongest of currencies, and the conviction spread in foreign financial circles that the only safe refuge for their funds was gold in their own vaults. These factors set in motion a run on the dollar from abroad, which will be described in the next chapter.

CHAPTER V.—RUNS ON THE DOLLAR

THE FIRST RUN IS MET

During September, 1931, while the Bank of England and the British government fought their desperate but losing battle for the maintenance of the gold standard, foreign owners of deposits in New York took alarm and withdrew funds from the United States on such a large scale as to necessitate gold exports of $254,000,000 in that one month. After the fall of the pound sterling, the run on the dollar increased to panic proportions. From all over the world came demands for gold in the United States, so that during the month of October alone the monetary stock of gold in the United States decreased by the unprecedented amount of $448,000,000. In the space of two months the United States lost $700,000,000 of gold, a greater loss of the precious metal than was suffered in any full year in all the eventful post-war history of the country.

The Federal Reserve authorities met the demand for gold without question. They pointed to the huge monetary stock of gold accumulated in the vaults of the Treasury and the Federal Reserve banks, and to the strength of the balance of international payments of the United States. They pointed out that a considerable part of the monetary stock of gold held in the United States was held in fact only in trust, being actually the property of foreign central banks owning balances here, and that our large surplus of gold was in any event of no particular advantage to this country. While the public at large became somewhat restive over the huge outflow of gold, the Federal Reserve authorities took the correct view and refused to share the apprehension of many financial leaders.

Although the Reserve Banks had no official relations with the Bank for International Settlements, the Federal Reserve Bank of New York thought it advisable to dispatch Mr. William Randolph Burgess, its Deputy Governor, to the meeting of the directors of the Bank for International Settlements held in October, 1931, to explain to them the international financial position of the United States. Newspaper dispatches from Geneva reported: "Mr. Burgess' explanation, which lasted more than one hour and a half . . . made an extremely good impression on his auditors, who included the governors of the central banks of France, Great Britain, Belgium, Germany, Switzerland, Holland, Sweden, and Italy." Several of these representatives of the leading central banks of the world expressed themselves as profoundly impressed and greatly comforted by the information disclosed by Mr. Burgess. The newspapers reported that "it became evident that any future attacks on the dollar will encounter strong opposition from the banks of issue."

This opposition on the part of the central banks to any future attacks on the dollar, and the spirit of coöperation which the various central banks of the world had so strongly professed during the entire post-war period, became strikingly conspicuous by their absence during the first half of 1932, when the individual institutions led by the Bank of France fairly outdid each other in their rush to convert their dollar balances into gold. Their hasty withdrawal of gold from the United States accelerated the run on the dollar, thereby frightening Americans as well as foreigners. The view gained ground that the representative of the Federal Reserve Bank of New York had protested too strongly, and that the Federal Reserve authorities had confessed their own weakness by finding it necessary to dispatch an emissary to Geneva to explain the American situation.

It was not the assurance given by the Federal Reserve officials, however, which brought to a temporary halt the run on the dollar. It was rather the prompt paying out of gold on the part of the Federal Reserve banks during September and October, 1931, and the fact that the people in the United States kept their heads and did not themselves clamor for gold. This attitude on the part of the people here alleviated fears of Europeans that the United States might follow the footsteps of Great Britain, and as a result during November and December, 1931, the monetary stock of gold of the country actually increased. The return flow of gold in November amounted to $122,000,000 and in December to about $46,000,000.

BANK FAILURES SHAKE CONFIDENCE

But even as the drain from abroad subsided, the financial structure of this country continued to be shaken by the failures of hundreds of banks. In the month of October, 1931, alone, 522 banks closed their doors, and in the six month period September, 1931, to February, 1932, inclusive, 1,823 banks failed, tying up deposits of $1,326,183,000, depriving depositors of their working capital, and causing hardship and despair throughout the length and breadth of the land. The causes of these failures we have discussed in preceding chapters.

Washington decided that something had to be done. In the first week of October, 1931, leading bankers were called in for a conference with the President and Treasury officials. The Administration succeeded in obtaining from the large and strong banks promise of assistance for the weaker ones through the formation of the National Credit Corporation, but only after the bankers had been assured that as soon as Congress convened a government institution would be formed to take over the work of the corporation set up by the bankers. This promise was carried out on January 22, 1932, when the law authorizing the creation of the Reconstruction Finance Corporation was enacted.

While the newspapers throughout this country heralded the birth of the National Credit Corporation and the establishment of the Reconstruction Finance Corporation as assuring the solution of our banking difficulties, public confidence was only partially restored. European bankers were not only skeptical of these measures, but actually viewed them with alarm. The French press was particularly critical, and its comments served to further undermine European confidence in the American dollar and in American finance. Paris newspapers interpreted the creation of the National Credit Corporation as official admission of a critical banking situation, and held that the discounting by the corporation of bank assets not eligible at the Reserve banks was an inflationary measure which would force the departure of the dollar from the gold standard. One paper carried a headline, "Not knowing how to get out of difficulties the United States goes joyously toward inflation." In London, the *Daily Mail* advised in headlines, "Sell Dollar and Franc Securities."

The net result of these events was a renewal of the run on the dollar toward the end of the year, although on a much smaller scale than in

September and October 1931. Foreigners again withdrew their funds in gold, and the outflow was increased by a flight of capital as many timid Americans, fearing abandonment of gold conversion, began to transfer funds abroad. The heavy demand for foreign currencies was reflected in a rise of the pound sterling from $3.25 in December, 1931, to $3.80 in April, 1932.

THE 1932 RUN

The suicide in March, 1932, of Ivar Kreuger, now revealed as an international embezzler and manipulator on a gigantic scale, added to the case of nerves from which financial centers suffered. His assistance to France, Germany and a number of other countries had been hailed by the leading bankers and statesmen of the world as financial achievements second only to those of the League of Nations. The collapse of his house of cards, built on false balance sheets and forgery, struck a body blow to the reputation of one of the best known of American investment banking houses. So great was the confidence in Kreuger that shrewd Yankee bankers not only distributed securities of his companies in amounts totalling some three hundred millions of dollars, but actually invested their own money in these securities in substantial amounts. The collapse of Kreuger & Toll, with resultant enormous losses to American investors, was one of the first shocks of the

G

many that were to undermine confidence in our financial leadership.

Although the Kreuger & Toll affair caused considerable commotion, it alone did not increase appreciably the run on the dollar. But suddenly, in May, withdrawals of gold assumed large proportions once again as foreigners took fright at financial developments within the United States. In April the Federal Reserve Board embarked on its famous easy money policy, buying government securities during May at the rate of $100,000,000 a week. A more alarming event was the passage by the House of Representatives of the so-called Goldsborough bill, directing the Federal Reserve Board to take the necessary steps to raise prices to the level of 1926. Although this bill was killed in the Senate, it clearly indicated that the noisy agitation for inflation was being taken seriously in Congress. At the same time, the inability of Congress to balance the budget, the agitation for payment of the soldiers' bonus, even in new fiat money, and the increased volume of short-term borrowing by the Treasury all contributed to the growing distrust of the dollar in Europe.

The reaction in Europe is clearly indicated in the following dispatch to the *New York Times* from Basle, Switzerland, on May 8, 1932:

"Reports brought by central bank governors to their meeting here to-day preliminary to the annual assembly of the stockholders of the Bank for International Settlements indicate that banking and commercial institutions of many European countries are now declining to accept dollars.

"Because of the Europeans' view of the difficulties of the United States Government in obtaining a balanced budget and the reports of the Goldsborough bill and rumors of impending inflation, they are hesitating to accept payment in dollars regardless of the opinion of financial leaders that fears of inflation in the United States are unfounded.

"The World Bank received numerous queries in the past week from bankers in all European countries concerning the United States situation and the stability of American currency."

The *Paris Journal des Debats* said editorially:

"The purchase by the Federal Reserve of Treasury bonds has resulted in weakness of the dollar, and that was the subject of telephone conferences of the directors of the Federal Reserve Board with the principal European banks of issue as well as the question of the international application of the policy of credit expansion."

During May alone, $214,000,000 of gold was withdrawn from the United States, and in June the monetary stock of gold in the United States decreased by approximately $234,000,000. Not only did foreign banks, and particularly central banks, withdraw their balances from the United States in the form of gold, but even individuals in many European countries who for years had hoarded American paper currency as the safest means of preserving their assets threw their precious dollar holdings on the market at any price. Shipments of American paper money from Europe during May and June, 1932, amounted to $10,938,000 and $16,253,000 respectively, as compared with net shipments of $467,000 and $8,032,000 during the same two months in the previous year.

THE DOLLAR'S STRENGTH

The faith in the dollar, which throughout the post-war period had bordered on religious belief, now showed quite distinct and general signs of weakening. Pending abandonment of the gold standard by the United States became common talk. So-called confidential reports emanated from Washington that plans had already been adopted for the devaluation of the currency. Bets were made in Wall Street at odds of one to three that before the end of June the United States would be off the gold standard.

Throughout this period of fear for the stability of the dollar, however, few people realized that no purely foreign influence was at all likely to force the United States to abandon the gold standard. In spite of net gold exports aggregating approximately $1,100,000,000 during the ten months from September, 1931, to June, 1932, the country nevertheless had left a monetary gold stock of fully $3,919,000,000 on the latter date. What some of our leading financiers and a great many other people forgot was that the balance of payments of the United States was basically favorable, apart from temporary shifts of liquid balances, that month after month the foreign trade of the United States showed an excess of exports over imports, and that each month substantial sums in the form of interest and principal were being paid to the United States on loans issued in previous years.

It was obvious to every careful observer that the moment the foreign short-term balances had been withdrawn or reduced to the absolute minimum, the loss of gold would come to an end. It was evident at the time that no foreign enemies could force the United States to devalue or depreciate its currency; only an internal run could force us off the gold standard. This was borne out in February and March, 1933, for only then, when the enemies from within were besieging the gates of the Federal Reserve Bank clamoring for their gold, did it become necessary finally to abandon the gold standard.

But in 1932 the gold bug had not as yet stung the average American. Although some frightened citizens continued to convert their deposits into gold or to transfer them into foreign currencies, their number was small. So implicit was the belief of the average American in the strength of the dollar, so deep rooted his faith in the preservation of our gold standard, that the fear which seized some Wall Street denizens left him cool. So long as foreigners, and particularly foreign central banks, were converting their deposits into gold, the end of the run on the dollar was merely a question of time, for the foreign balances in New York were not large.

WHY FRANCE DREW GOLD

It is notable that about two-thirds of the gold exported during this period went to France, that country absorbing $782,000,000 of American gold in the year ending June 30, 1932. However, one cannot blame the French for taking their money home in the form of gold. The depreciation of the pound sterling had cost the Bank of France 2,432,000,000 francs, or about $92,000,000. This loss more than wiped out the actual capital and surplus of the Bank of France, making necessary assistance by the government which, with the Amortization Office, assumed the loss suffered by the central bank. It is not surprising, therefore, to find that institution using all the means at its disposal to prevent further losses of the kind. In its report for 1931 the Bank of France explained its actions in the following frank and candid manner:

"The progressive liquidation of the artificial currency systems, on the putting into force of which so much effort was spent since the war, marks a decisive stage on the road to economic purification. We have always refused to adhere to these easy solutions, of which we perceived the dangers. We have made our action conform to the hard lessons of experience, whereas opinion is often attracted by the mirage of seductive conceptions whose factitious character and inefficacy reveal themselves upon contact with realities. More than ever we are convinced that it is our duty to secure the metallic basis of the franc, which is the only stable foundation on which a currency can be supported. We regard convertibility into gold not as an antiquated form of slavery but as a necessary discipline. We see in it the only effective guaranty of the security of contracts and business ethics."

At the same time the resentment felt throughout the United States against France is understandable. France, a country which had obtained generous assistance from the United States government during and after the war, whose government owed the United States government $3,921,500,000 and had received substantial reduction in interest on this debt, was withdrawing gold at a time when it was most embarrassing to the United States. The American critic did not remember the previous experience of the French in London and did not consider the old saying that the burned child dreads the fire, nor that even with these withdrawals the gold stock in the United States still represented almost one-third of the total monetary stock of gold of the world. He merely felt that France, no longer "the most beloved nation on earth," was draining the gold reserves of his country at a most inopportune time.

END OF THE GOLD EXCHANGE STANDARD

The example of France was followed by others. The gold exchange standard, which had been the mainstay of post-war stabilization, practically disappeared overnight. It had been based on the presumption that reserves in foreign exchange were the equivalent of gold; that they were in effect "interest-bearing gold." This presumption had proved false, and believers of the myth who had kept their reserves in pounds thus sustained heavy losses. The various foreign central banks were not slow in showing their disillusionment. The National Bank of Switzerland reduced its foreign exchange holdings from 566,582,000 Swiss francs on September 15, 1931, to 103,974,000 francs at the end of the year, and to 56,000,000 francs by the end of June, 1932. Similarly, the Nederlandsche Bank, which as a result of the depreciation of the pound sterling had lost about 30,000,000 florins or $12,000,000, not only changed its president but also its policies concerning foreign exchange holdings. Its holdings of foreign bills, which on September 21 had amounted to 231,206,000 florins, decreased to 68,632,000 florins on June 27, 1932. In the case of both the Nederlandsche Bank and the Swiss National Bank, the notes in circulation were almost fully covered by gold after such repatriation of reserves.

The principal countries which withdrew gold from the United States during the period September, 1931, to June, 1932, and the amounts withdrawn each month, are shown below:

(In thousands of dollars)

1931	*France*	*Belgium*	*Holland*	*Switzerland*
September	$ 24,087	.....	$ 4,172	$ 349
October	324,500	$ 9,678	35,904	17,617
November	10	57	394	515
December	15,150	5,861	9,857	1,270
1932				
January	83,783	12,553	6,257	1,759
February	98,203	17,859	8,672	254
March	37,532	6,341	.....	6
April	24,527	669	18,707	115
May	63,216	19,930	58,473	53,554
June	111,411	26,250	23,168	62,603
Total	$782,419	$99,198	$165,604	$138,042

Even Germany, which owed huge amounts of short-term credits to banks in the United States frozen by standstill agreements, withdrew $3,000,000 in May and about $10,000,000 in June. Here was the spectacle of citizens of a country whose central bank owed the Federal Reserve banks $25,000,000, which through depreciation of the pound reduced its short-term debt to England about 30 per cent, and in whose favor President Hoover had invoked the moratorium on war debts and reparations, showing their gratitude by withdrawing gold.

The large withdrawals of gold from the United States, the practical abandonment of the gold exchange standard and the desire of each central bank to convert its foreign exchange resources into gold further intensified the economic and financial crisis throughout the world. The amount of international credit available to finance international trade was greatly curtailed, affecting adversely not only the movement of commodities between countries but also prices. The collapse of 1931 and the panic-stricken demand for gold on the part of all central banks of the world brought the international financial situation back to where it was shortly after the war, with this distinction, that the world in 1932 was confronted with the additional task of liquidating the huge volume of short- and long-term foreign credits contracted prior to 1930.

THE RUSH TO HOARD

The conflagration in the international money markets, which early in 1931 might have been localized, pending correction of major problems, by concerted action on the part of the few leading countries, spread rapidly from one country to another. Started by the collapse of the Credit Anstalt, the flames swept rapidly over the continent of Europe, leaving havoc and destruction in their wake. They crossed the English Channel and, after forcing Great Britain off the gold standard and causing huge losses to those who had maintained balances in London, spread to the United States, where they burnt away the foundations of an already badly shaken financial and economic structure.

Fear-stricken creditors throughout the world displayed a frantic desire to withdraw their funds, regardless of the possibility of payment. The financial position of the debtor was ignored. Gold became an international fetish, the one safe investment, and a maddened world rushed to turn claims of all kinds into the yellow metal. Creditors disregarded completely the fact that only comparatively small, marginal sums can be transferred, either within a country or internationally, or from one form of investment to another, without wreaking havoc. Banks and private firms the world over were racing madly to increase their liquidity and to strengthen their cash position at any cost. Gilt-edged securities were thrown on the market at sacrifice prices in order to obtain cash assets. Forced sales disorganized the stock exchanges, many of which abroad were closed after the suspension of the gold standard by Great Britain.

Distress and fear possessed the people of debtor and creditor countries alike, and caused hoarding of gold and currencies on a large scale. The sharp increase in the circulation of notes of large denominations in France and in Switzerland, in the face of falling commodity prices and a shrinking volume of trade and employment, proves beyond doubt that the notes were not issued in response to the needs of business but were absorbed by hoarding. The note circulation of the Bank of France increased during the period from January 1, 1929, to December 31, 1931, by 21,366,000,000 francs, of which 16,609,000,000 francs were accounted for by an increase in 1,000 franc notes. Some of these notes probably were bought by foreigners who feared for the stability of their own currencies. In Switzerland notes of 1,000- and 500-franc denominations made up almost one-third of the total note circulation in 1931, whereas in 1930 they represented less than one-fifth. The export of Swiss notes abroad assumed such proportions that the National Bank of Switzerland requested the commercial banks to exercise restraint in delivering bank notes to foreigners, and it was only the cooperation of these institutions that made an embargo on the export of notes unnecessary. Even in countries threatened with currency depreciation hoarding of currency took place on a large scale.

In the United States the large number of bank failures and the disturbing rumors in connection with the continuous outflow of gold caused growing uneasiness on the part of the public, which manifested itself in increasing withdrawals of currency for hoarding. Total money in circulation increased from $4,890,123,348 at the end of 1930 to $5,695,000,000 at the end of June, 1932, an increase of about 16 per cent during a period when payrolls were drastically reduced, when wholesale prices had fallen by about 20 per cent and general business activity had contracted by 21 per cent.

To the individual, hoarding of money is simply a measure of self-protection in critical times at the cost of lost interest, but the cumulative effect of currency hoarding on the national economy of a country is far-reaching. The banks are forced to increase their liquidity through the sale of assets in rapidly declining markets, which in turn leads to further bank failures and thus to further hoarding. The hoarding of currency constitutes a drain on the credit base of the country, tending to bring about contraction of credit with resulting adverse effects on industry and trade. Although the effects of hoarding can be counteracted by open market operations on the part of central banks, as happened in this country during 1932, the influence on the banking system is serious nevertheless. It discourages banks from making loans and makes them seek only the most liquid type of investment, regardless of the rate of interest earned.

FINANCIAL NATIONALISM DEVELOPS

The international loss of confidence started a flight of capital into a few stable countries. It caused funds to flow from centers where high rates of interest were paid to centers where extremely low rates prevailed, a movement quite abnormal and illogical. At a time when debtor nations had to adopt various and sundry artificial expedients to provide credit for financing their industry and trade, the idle funds of countries like France, Holland and Switzerland accumulated steadily. Interest rates in the so-called gold countries declined rapidly, thereby contrasting sharply with the rates in debtor countries. These low rates of interest, while indicating an abundance of surplus funds, also reflected the unwillingness of bankers to lend on anything but the safest kind of collateral. Thus, for example, at the end of April, 1932, the Paris money market suffered from a super-abundance of short-term funds seeking liquid and ultra-conservative investments, and at the same time from lack of credits to finance ordinary business.

This international movement of funds against the normal currents and in complete disregard of interest rates indicated that the international money market had ceased to function. It was the full realization of this fact, plus the various currency restrictions imposed by most countries, that finally induced the financial authorities in debtor countries to bring about a reduction in interest rates in their own markets, irrespective of their currency position. The actions of the various central banks were determined exclusively by domestic considerations without regard to their possible effect on other nations. Each country affected by the panic adopted measures best suited to its needs to stem the tide of deflation and to remove the débris caused by the economic and financial collapse.

The runs on the dollar, the complete breakdown of the international money market and the abandonment of the gold standard, *de facto* or legally, by most countries of the world, brought to an end the era of stable currencies. They destroyed once and for all belief that currency stabilization or the gold standard could be maintained in an economically unbalanced world. They revealed in a glaring light the great damage caused by the war and its aftermath, and they put before the world once again the problem, made familiar after the war, of currency stabilization. With the assistance of American capital, drifting currencies had in previous years been anchored to the buoy of the gold dollar. When this buoy itself threatened to begin to float, the currencies, with few exceptions, tore themselves from their moorings and became mere playthings on the waves of the ocean of fluctuating economic and financial forces.

The situation in 1932 seemed far more difficult than that at the end of the war. Then there were many illusions extant about the gold standard. The financial leaders in the United States and Europe were still deeply rooted in the pre-war conception of the gold standard, and cherished the belief that once a currency is stabilized, manipulation of the central bank's discount rate will be sufficient to maintain the stability of that currency. They did not realize that the world had changed. They were fighting windmills in Don Quixote fashion and the American loans were the spears in their hands. The moment American investors refused to lend their money throughout the world, the mirage disappeared and the desert of devastation caused by the war and especially the disastrous peace-time policies stood revealed.

EFFECTS ON THE UNITED STATES

The run on the dollar by the European countries caused grave financial unsettlement in the United States. But in spite of the statement of President Hoover that at one time the United

States was within two weeks of the abandonment of the gold standard, it must be emphatically denied that throughout 1932 the stability of the dollar was ever threatened. All the world could not have forced the United States to abandon the gold standard; only a loss of nerve by Americans could have forced its abandonment, and in spite of the intensification of the depression they made no heavy demands for gold during 1932.

However, the strain of the gold withdrawals and the deepening gloom in business circles did have a profound effect on our financial structure. Securities were thrown on the market irrespective of value and their prices declined sharply. Banks throughout the country continued to fail in rapid succession and this in turn caused a substantial increase in the hoarding of currency.

As security prices declined the extension of credit practically came to a halt. Week after week the reporting member bank figures indicated a further contraction in the amount of loans of all types. While all kinds of loans and investments were sharply reduced the amount of government securities held by the banks increased. It was remarkable indeed that, at a period when everybody talked of inflation and of the abandonment of the gold standard, the banks should put more money in government securities, an investment which is usually adversely affected by a major depreciation of the currency.

H

Further recession in business under the circumstances prevailing during the first part of the year was inevitable. Commodity prices, which during the latter part of 1931 had remained more or less stable, resumed their decline and the Bureau of Labor Statistics index fell from 70 in November, 1931, to 64 in June, 1932. Economic and financial conditions in the United States in June were at a very low ebb.

But at this time a series of events and developments occurred which brought about a marked change in public psychology. Congress adjourned after passing a bill to increase taxes, thus giving promise of a more nearly balanced budget. Its adjournment eliminated the threat of unsound and inflationary legislation. At Lausanne Germany's creditors reached an agreement which practically eliminated the reparations problem and held out prospects of effective future coöperation among the statesmen of Europe. Finally, the means and measures adopted by the government, particularly the operations of the Reconstruction Finance Corporation, began to have an effect. Gradually hope replaced fear and the horizon began to brighten. Was this hope based on realities? The answer would depend upon the effectiveness of the measures adopted by the government.

CHAPTER VI.—SHOTS IN THE ARM

THE NATIONAL CREDIT CORPORATION

The alarming number of bank failures during the autumn of 1931 and the growing mistrust of the dollar abroad induced the government, after a long period of inaction, difficult to understand or condone, to take cognizance of the adverse banking situation and to adopt remedies for buttressing the collapsing unit banking system. No broad vision in their concept of the problem was manifested by our then leaders, however. They believed even then that bank failures were a passing phase caused by poor business conditions, and particularly by the temporary panic fright of the people. They proceeded on the assumption that, if some scheme could be invented to restore confidence, our financial troubles would disappear and the banks could continue to operate as before. In spite of the fact that the investigations of the Glass sub-committee in the Senate had fully revealed the weaknesses of the banking system, no definite program was suggested by the Administration or by the bankers for its reorganization.

One of the first steps taken by the Administration to shore up the collapsing unit banking system was the creation on October 13, 1931, of the

National Credit Corporation. If any action was near-sighted and doomed to failure from the beginning, it was this. In retrospect, it would appear that the National Credit Corporation was not created for the purpose of actually helping the banks, for it is obvious from its charter that it could not serve effectively even as a temporary relief measure. It was intended primarily as a psychological trick to alleviate the fears of depositors and to make them believe that the banks of the country, by acting in unison, could bolster up the many weak spots in the banking structure.

Briefly stated, the National Credit Corporation was organized and operated as follows: The Corporation obtained funds with which to make loans to individual banks needing aid through subscriptions to its renewable gold notes, which it was authorized to issue up to one billion dollars. Each bank was asked to subscribe to the notes to the extent of 2 per cent of its net demand and time deposits.

Banks subscribing to these notes organized themselves into associations, of which one or more were set up in each Federal Reserve District. If a bank needed a loan it was to make an application to the Association of which it was a member. This Association appointed a loan committee to pass on the loans requested by its members and, if the loan was approved locally, it was recommended to the loan committee of the National

Credit Corporation, which then actually made the advance.

Each loan to an individual bank was evidenced by the bank's own note adequately secured by collateral. Each loan was, in addition, a joint liability of the other banks in the local Association as well. Furthermore, the total amount of loans which could be made to all the banks in one district was limited to the subscriptions of all the banks in that district to the notes of the National Credit Corporation, except that loans in excess of the aggregate subscriptions could be made provided the banks of the association gave their consent and each bank became liable for its *pro rata* share of the excess loan. Thus, for example, if the banks in the Federal Reserve District of San Francisco had subscribed to $30,000,000 of the notes of the National Credit Corporation, the total amount of loans that could be obtained by banks in that district could not exceed $30,000,000, unless loans above this amount were assumed directly by all the banks of the association.

The plan of the National Credit Corporation was one of mutual assistance by the banks themselves. As the corporation was organized, however, it was obvious that such assistance could be very small. In the first place, few banks cared, even in an emergency, to notify all other banks in its district that it was in difficulties, and to have its books examined by its competitors. Also, the fact that the banks in each association were jointly liable for advances made to its members made the associations quite hesitant in approving such loans. Furthermore, the provision that the amount of loans made to one district must not exceed the total subscription by all the banks of that district limited the amount of funds which could be placed at the disposal of banks in districts where help was especially needed.

Although the National Credit Corporation was hailed by the Administration and the press as a great achievement, banks continued to fail in increasing numbers and, as a matter of fact during October, 1931, the month that the National Credit Corporation came into existence, no less than 522 banks closed their doors. Bank failures during November and December as well continued very heavy. The magic trick with which the Administration sought to blind the eyes of the frightened depositors did not work. Throughout its entire life the National Credit Corporation called on the subscribers to its notes to pay in a total of only $135,000,000, a mere drop in the bucket when compared with the magnitude of the situation.

NEW VALUATIONS FOR OLD BONDS

In the meantime the continued decline in bond prices placed the banks throughout the country in a difficult position. If their bonds were valued at market prices in examination by Federal or state authorities, they would have to recognize losses which in many instances would have wiped out their surplus and in not a few cases even their capital. To remedy this situation, the Comptroller of the Currency in the last week of December, 1931, addressed a letter to all national banks informing them officially that bonds enjoying the four highest ratings of any standard rating service, would be valued at cost because of the prevailing low market prices. "What we are always interested in," said Comptroller John W. Pole, "is the solvency of banks and not necessarily their liquidity. There are many fine companies which have issued bonds and there is every reason to believe they will meet their interest charges and pay their principal at maturity. Why should we ignore those facts and take quotations from a blackboard in a market where there are all sellers and no buyers? We wish to protect banks that have bought good bonds from any such situation, and while every case will have to stand on its own merits, it is our plan to regard intrinsic value as the real basis for valuing the securities held by banks."

This step of the Comptroller of the Currency was in perfect harmony with the "shot in the arm" policy of an Administration which refused to read the handwriting on the wall. It ignored realities and believed in magic formulæ to bring back the prosperity that was constantly lurking around the corner. During the period of general distrust in banking, liquidity is imperative unless liberal access can be had to rediscounting agencies. Arguments about solvency and intrinsic value never succeeded in stopping a run. Only by paying on demand can a bank regain the confidence of its depositors. The Comptroller's examiners, in the case of the banks which readily availed themselves of his instructions, thus did not recognize the true position of a number of banks. Less generous valuations of assets would have shown not only lack of liquidity but also lack of solvency. State banking authorities followed suit.

THE RECONSTRUCTION FINANCE CORPORATION

The situation called for immediate Congressional action, and on January 22, 1932, the Reconstruction Finance Corporation was established. The Administration finally realized that, in order to prevent banks from failing, substantial loans would have to be granted them. The philosophy of "rugged individualism" and the ancient slogan of "keep government out of business" were sacrificed, in view of the approaching presidential election and the need for finally showing some constructive action and achievements. A way was found to socialize the losses that had occurred, and to perpetuate a moribund system of unit banks and over-mortgaged railroads with the taxpayers' money.

The Reconstruction Finance Corporation was

established with a capital of $500,000,000, entirely subscribed by the government. The resources of the Corporation could be increased by the issue of bonds to the extent of three times its capital, so that the total resources originally at the disposal of the Reconstruction Finance Corporation amounted to $2,000,000,000. The Reconstruction Finance Corporation is entirely a government institution. Its board of directors is composed of the Secretary of the Treasury or his representative, the Governor of the Federal Reserve Board and the Farm Loan Commissioner, who are ex-officio members, and four other members appointed by the President.

The Reconstruction Finance Corporation was not intended to aid commercial banks exclusively. Its facilities were placed at the disposal of various kinds of financial institutions, such as commercial banks, savings banks, building and loan associations, etc. It could make loans also, upon the recommendation of the Interstate Commerce Commission, to railways which could not otherwise obtain funds, and it was authorized to accept drafts arising out of an export of goods actually sold. All loans made by the Reconstruction Finance Corporation had to be fully secured, and the law further stated that no obligation of foreign governments or of foreign corporations could be used as collateral for loans from the Reconstruction Finance Corporation.

With two billion dollars at its disposal, the Reconstruction Finance Corporation was in a position to make huge sums available to weakened banks throughout the country. From the day of its organization to July 21, 1932, the Reconstruction Finance Corporation authorized loans aggregating $1,172,000,000, of which $703,000,000 or 60 per cent was made available to banks and trust companies, about $65,000,000 to building and loan associations, $65,000,000 to insurance companies and $80,000,000 to mortgage loan companies. The total amount of loans authorized up to July 21, 1932 is shown in the table below:

Banks and trust companies	$ 702,942,914
Building and loan associations	64,710,783
Insurance companies	65,051,500
Mortgage loan companies	79,972,000
Credit unions	405,000
Federal land banks	26,000,000
Joint stock land banks	1,330,000
Agricultural credit corporations	662,914
Live-stock credit corporations	7,496,086
Railroads	223,412,109
Total	$1,171,983,306

The effect of the establishment and operation of the Reconstruction Finance Corporation was direct and immediate. The number of bank failures decreased very sharply, and during the month of March fell to 48, one of the smallest numbers reported during any month for several years. Any commercial bank confronted with a run could pledge collateral with the Reconstruction Finance Corporation and immediately obtain assistance from it. The establishment of the Reconstruction Finance Corporation changed the attitude of depositors toward their banks. From now on it was believed that the Reconstruction Finance Corporation, with the huge resources at its disposal, could definitely prevent bank failures. This changed attitude immediately restored the confidence of the public in the banks, and the decline in deposits ceased.

A PERIOD OF LOST OPPORTUNITIES

While the real merits of the Reconstruction Finance Corporation cannot be denied, it is obvious that it could act only as a sedative. It could be considered only as a temporary emergency measure, for its success depended on further legislation looking toward the reorganization and strengthening of the entire banking system of the country. Instead of taking adequate measures to reorganize the banks during the period of quiet in which the sedative rested the nerves of the people throughout the country, the Administration stood still and rested on its laurels. Its spokesmen pointed out with great pride that bank failures had almost come to a halt. Newspaper headlines in bold type shouted the fact that the banking crisis had been overcome and that bank failures had come to an end.

Were not the authorities aware that each loan to an individual bank had to be secured, and that the operation of the Reconstruction Finance Corporation had deprived the banks of some of their best assets? Why did they not consider what would happen to banks confronted with additional withdrawals of deposits after most of their good assets had already been pledged as collateral for loans from the Reconstruction Finance Corporation? This obvious fact apparently did not enter the minds of the Administration. The Happiness Boys in Washington put the temporary success of the Reconstruction Finance Corporation on a big drum, and from the rugged coast of Maine to sunny California speakers and propagandists heralded the great achievement.

The Reconstruction Finance Corporation offered the Administration a period of rest during which to reorganize and permanently strengthen the banking structure of the country. Looking backward, the entire period from February, 1932, to the end of the Hoover Administration may be termed "a period of lost opportunities." But, as it was, the Reconstruction Finance Corporation poured many hundreds of millions of dollars into the coffers of the banks, insurance companies and railroads, and by the end of 1932 the total amounted to the staggering sum of $1,937,000,000. True, banks did not fail to the same extent as they had in the fall of 1931. True, many banks, and particularly the large ones throughout the country, were placed in a position to cover all their deposits by cash obtained through loans from the Reconstruction Finance Corporation. The very operation of the Reconstruction Finance Corporation, however, carried the germ of disease and destruction in it. It was obvious that the moment banks had no more collateral to offer to the Reconstruction Finance Corporation and one of the larger ones failed, the entire myth that bank failures had ended would disappear and the panic would break out again, with accelerated and renewed force.

BABY BONDS

By the time the Reconstruction Finance Corporation had begun to function, the hoarding of currency had reached alarming proportions and the Administration sought means of combating it.

On February 3, 1932, the President issued a statement appealing to the people to cease hoarding of currency as a patriotic duty to the country. On February 6, representatives of 42 civic organizations with a membership of over 20,000,000 met in conference with the President, the Secretary of the Treasury, the President of the Reconstruction Finance Corporation and other officials, and decided on a national anti-hoarding campaign under the leadership of Colonel Frank Knox, publisher of the *Chicago Daily News*. On March 6 the campaign was officially launched with nationwide radio messages by the President, the Secretary of the Treasury, the President of the Reconstruction Finance Corporation and the Chairman of the Citizens Reconstruction Organization.

The Secretary of the Treasury in his address announced the sale of new 2 per cent Treasury Certificates maturing March 15, 1933, in denominations of $50, $100 and $500, which came to be known popularly as "Baby Bonds." These certificates were redeemable before maturity at the option of the holder at par plus accrued interest, upon sixty days' notice. The object was to induce frightened hoarders to invest buried dollars in government securities and thus return idle currency to circulation. It was hoped that no money deposited in banks or otherwise invested would be used to buy the Baby Bonds, but that they would simply lure dollars from their hiding places. Said the Secretary of the Treasury, "As a matter of enlightened self-interest, every one who holds these idle dollars should put them back to work through the placing of deposits with sound banking institutions or through the purchase of sound investments. I cannot assume to advise as to which method should be selected."

Was not this statement a startling and shocking, although indirect, admission that some of the banks might not be sound? Was a 2 per cent certificate, redeemable at sixty days' notice, a special inducement to hoarders while Postal Saving certificates, payable on demand, were allowing the same rate of interest and while one-year certificates sold by the Treasury as part of its March 15, 1932, financing bore interest at 3¾ per cent? The Baby Bonds were another step in the series of devices designed to rebuild public confidence by magic tricks. The total amount of Baby Bonds sold was only $35,000,000.

THE GLASS-STEAGALL BILL

While the Reconstruction Finance Corporation temporarily stemmed the tide of banking failures, large withdrawals of gold from the United States began to have their effect on the Federal Reserve System, and it became necessary to amend the Federal Reserve Act so that the huge gold reserves in the United States could be utilized to their full advantage in expanding credit at home. The Glass-Steagall bill was passed on February 27, 1932, to achieve this.

Up to that time the Federal Reserve Act had required that Federal Reserve notes be secured by gold to the extent of not less than 40 per cent and by eligible paper for the balance up to 100 per cent.

All notes of the Federal Reserve banks outstanding and not covered in part by eligible paper had to be secured 100 per cent by gold. On February 29, 1932, the total amount of notes issued by the Federal Reserve agents to the Federal Reserve banks amounted to $2,911,743,000, secured by $892,153,000 in eligible paper and the balance by gold. The small volume of eligible paper rediscounted at that time gave the Reserve banks an inadequate supply to put behind circulating notes. Thus it happened that, prior to the passage of the Glass-Steagall bill, the actual gold cover of the Federal Reserve notes amounted to 76 per cent instead of the statutory minimum of 40 per cent.

To remedy this situation the Federal Reserve Act was amended by the Glass-Steagall bill. It authorized the Reserve banks to consider government securities purchased by them in the open market as equivalent to eligible paper. Its chief value was to permit the Reserve banks to pledge government securities acquired in the open market as well as eligible paper as cover for their notes, thereby making it unnecessary for them to have gold in excess of 40 per cent of outstanding notes in the event of a shortage of eligible commercial paper. This provision of the Glass-Steagall bill, although criticized by some as a step towards fiat money, must be considered under the existing circumstances to have been a sound measure. It freed the Reserve banks completely from any danger that might have arisen from withdrawals of gold by foreign nations, and enabled them to buy government bonds freely in the open market and thus to offset the effects on the market of an outflow of gold. By making it possible for the Federal Reserve banks to consider government securities as equivalent to eligible paper, the so-called free gold of the reserve banks, that held in excess of minimum reserve requirements, was largely increased.

The other provisions of the Glass-Steagall bill liberalized the regulations of the Federal Reserve Act governing loans to member banks. A new section was added authorizing loans to groups of five or more member banks, or fewer if they had ten per cent of the deposits in their Reserve district, secured by collateral otherwise not acceptable as security for advances. The amendment also permitted individual banks capitalized at $5,000,000 or less to obtain loans on collateral ineligible under other provisions of the Act. Although the amount of loans made under this amendment has never been published, it is understood that comparatively few loans were made to groups of banks because of the difficulty of finding five banks which would be willing to mutually guarantee their obligations at the Reserve bank. It was clear that banks would rather endeavor to obtain loans from the Reconstruction Finance Corporation than to approach their competitors and disclose their difficulties to them. However, it is likely that some smaller banks borrowed extensively under the provision, particularly during the first two months of 1933.

The liberalization of the lending powers of the Federal Reserve banks was carried a step further by the Emergency Relief and Reconstruction Act of July 21, 1932, which permitted individuals, partnerships and corporations to borrow directly from the Federal Reserve banks provided the borrower could prove that he could not obtain the accommodation from commercial banks. This provision was an innovation in the central banking history of the United States, in that for the first time it opened the facilities of the Federal Reserve System to individuals directly. It was of quite minor practical importance, however, because it was obvious that any individual in possession of eligible paper or government securities could obtain a loan from a commercial bank. The primary purpose of the law was to help individuals, partnerships and corporations, other than banks, in cities or districts where there were no banking facilities. Very little use has been made of this provision by individuals.

Taken together, the Glass-Steagall bill and the Reconstruction Finance Corporation were desirable measures taken to meet an emergency. The Reconstruction Finance Corporation provided funds to banks throughout the country, while the Glass-Steagall bill strengthened the Federal Reserve banks and enabled them to part with large amounts of gold without in any way being forced to contract their activities. If these measures had been looked upon as mere emergency measures, and steps had been taken at the same time to reorganize and reconstruct the banking system of the country permanently, the collapse of 1933 could have been avoided. But, as was stated before, it proved to be a period of lost opportunities.

FEDERAL RESERVE OPEN MARKET OPERATIONS

The Federal Reserve banks, having been freed from the shackles of an inadequate supply of eligible paper to cover their outstanding notes, now inaugurated open market operations on a scale unprecedented in the history of any central bank. They sought thus to offset the losses of gold and the increased volume of currency in circulation, by providing banks with large amounts of reserves made available as the Reserve banks paid for the government bonds they bought with checks on themselves. The government security holdings of the Reserve banks, which on February 24, 1932, amounted to $741,000,000, grew rapidly and by the end of June, 1932, amounted to $1,801,000,000, an increase of $1,060,000,000.

The shot-in-the-arm method was now going at full blast. Discounts of the member banks at the Reserve banks decreased from $835,000,000 on

February 24 to $470,000,000 on June 29, 1932. Prime bankers' acceptances, which in March of 1932 had been selling at a discount of between 2⅜ to 2⅝ per cent, in June were selling at a discount of ⅞ of 1 per cent. United States Treasury notes and certificates of a maturity of 3 to 6 months, which during February were selling to yield 2.42 per cent, were quoted in June to yield 0.34 per cent. Member bank balances with the Reserve banks, which on February 24 amounted to $1,878,000,000, had increased to $2,034,000,000 on June 29, 1932, an increase of $156,000,000.

The objective of the huge open market operations of the Reserve banks therefore was twofold: one, to offset the outflow of gold and, two, to pump large amounts of reserve funds into the banks, so as to reduce interest rates and create extremely easy money market conditions. The first purpose of the Reserve banks was understandable, and was in line with their traditional policies. In previous years, when gold came to this country in large volume, the Federal Reserve banks usually counteracted the influence of the gold inflow by selling government securities or by not renewing bankers' acceptances held in their portfolio. It was natural therefore that, during a period when gold was leaving this country in large amounts, the Reserve banks should continue the same policy and offset this outflow of gold through purchases of securities in the open market.

In this connection it should be kept in mind, as far as the money market is concerned, that the purchase of government securities or acceptances by the Reserve banks in the open market has the same effect on the member banks as an inflow of gold. In each case, if not offset by other influences, the result is an increase in the balances of the member banks at the Reserve banks. Whenever the balances of the member banks with the Reserve banks exceed by considerable amounts the fixed legal reserve requirements, the banks are in an especially easy credit position.

The Reserve banks, by buying more government securities than was warranted by the outflow of gold and the hoarding of currency, however, worked on the assumption that an increase in the reserve balances of the member banks and the consequent lowering of interest rates would induce the banks to extend loans more freely to industry and trade. This aspect of the open market operations was definitely intended to increase the amount of bank credit outstanding and thereby check the continuing liquidation of securities and the continuing deflation of all kinds of values. In other words, the Federal Reserve authorities worked on the old theory that, in order to bring to a halt a period of falling prices and decreased business activity, the only thing necessary was to flood the market with money and the revival would automatically take place. The Reserve banks, however, made their calculations without giving full consideration to the attitude of the banks. Being fully aware of the nervousness of their depositors and the danger of extensive new bank failures, and realizing that a run on deposits might set in any day, they adhered to a policy of high liquidity. Not only did they not increase their loans, but the figures on "other" loans, which represent primarily commercial loans of the reporting member banks, showed a decrease from February 24 to June 29, 1932, of about $653,000,000.

In spite of the plethora of funds thus injected into the money market and the low rates of interest resulting, bond prices, apart from government issues, fell sharply. Whereas in February, 1932, the index of 60 high grade bond prices stood at 80.3, in June, 1932, the same index stood at 72.2, a clear indication that the banks throughout the country were taking no chances and that they were acquiring only such securities as could be converted into cash immediately at the Reserve banks. That this was the policy of the banks can also be seen from the fact that during the period under discussion the holdings of government securities of the reporting member banks increased by $448,000,000 in spite of the abnormally low yields on these bonds.

While the open market operations of the Reserve banks succeeded in bringing about a sharp reduction in interest rates and flooded the open market with short-term funds, they did not achieve their final aim. They did not bring about an increase in the volume of outstanding bank credit, and did not halt the decline in business activity and the persistent fall in prices of securities and commodities. It was a typical shot-in-the-arm method, to drug the patient and thus make him survive the painful process of liquidation which went on slowly but surely.

FEDERAL HOME LOAN BANKS

The program of the Administration, however, was not complete. It still had rabbits in its hat with which to startle the public into believing that its measures could permanently strengthen the financial structure of the country. One of these rabbits was the Federal Home Loan Bank Act, a measure so badly drawn that it was obvious to many from the beginning that it was doomed to fail. The Administration believed in it for a while, but even President Hoover, in one of his last messages to Congress, recommended the reorganization of his Home Loan Bank System.

The Administration believed that the various measures adopted by it had stemmed the tide of deflation. It did recognize, however, the continued overhanging menace of the mortgage system to the financial structure of the country. Throughout the entire post-war boom period the mortgage business had expanded rapidly, and building and loan associations, mortgage companies, savings banks, life insurance companies and individuals held billions of dollars of mortgage bonds and certificates. So long as the country enjoyed great prosperity, payment of principal and interest on mortgages was possible, even where loans were based on inflated values. The moment the real estate boom in the United States was over, however, it became obvious that many even of the so-called first mortgages represented non-existent values. Many real estate owners found themselves unable to meet the interest on their mortgages, and wholesale defaults on first mortgages and transfers of properties to the mortgagees set in. The Administration felt that something had to be done; but the mountain labored and brought forth only a mouse. Out of all the negotiations and discussions concerning a central mortgage bank for urban real estate, the Home Loan Bank System was evolved.

The Federal Home Loan Bank Act established twelve Federal Home Loan Banks, coördinated and supervised by a Federal Home Loan Bank Board. Each bank, covering a certain district, was intended to do business with the following types of institutions: building and loan associations, savings and loan associations, coöperative banks, homestead associations, insurance companies and savings banks. These institutions were to subscribe to the capital of the bank up to 1 per cent of the aggregate unpaid principal of their home mortgage loans. The amount not subscribed by the various institutions was to be furnished by the Treasury, which appropriated $125,000,000 for this purpose.

The Home Loan Banks were authorized to make advances against amortized (installment) home mortgages which ran for an original term of eight years or more. The advance might be up to 60 per cent of the unpaid principal of the home mortgage loan, but in no case could the advance by a Home Loan Bank exceed 40 per cent of the value of the real estate securing the home mortgage loan. If secured by a home mortgage given in respect of a home mortgage loan that runs for less than eight years, the advance might not be in excess of 50 per cent of the unpaid principal of the home mortgage loan nor exceed 30 per cent of the value of the real estate securing the home mortgage loan. The following example will clarify this provision: If a savings bank had granted a mortgage loan for $10,000 on a property and this mortgage ran for more than eight years, the savings bank might obtain from a Home Loan Bank an advance of $6,000, provided the $6,000 represented not more than 40 per cent of the value of the house mortgaged, which meant that the value of the house had to be at least $15,000. If the mortgage on the same property ran for less than eight years, then the savings bank might obtain an advance of only $4,500, or 30 per cent of the $15,000 assessed value of the property. The valuation of the real estate was to be determined at the time the advance was made.

No advance might be granted by a Home Loan Bank if the value of the property exceeded $20,000 or covered a property designed for more than three families. In order to increase the resources of the Home Loan Banks, the latter were authorized to issue debentures to be secured by eligible obligations of borrowing institutions.

This, briefly stated, was the new system which was to solve the real estate problem of the country. According to spokesmen of the Administration, it was intended to prevent widows and orphans from losing their mortgaged properties and to bring about a new era in real estate financing. It was again one of those measures intended primarily to have a psychological effect but which in themselves could do very little to remedy the situation. A careful analysis of the Home Loan Bank Act reveals clearly that the only function that the system could perform was to make moderate loans to building and loan associations, mortgage companies and savings banks on the very best mortgages held by them. That is the beginning and the end of the function of the Home Loan Bank System. Although considerable propaganda was broadcast in favor of the Home Loan

Banks, comparatively few institutions eligible for membership availed themselves of this privilege and no debenture issues were offered to the public. The first loan of the system was approved on November 29, 1932, but since then little has been heard of the entire business. Considering the amount of first mortgages on houses outstanding and the magnitude of the real estate problem which confronted the nation, the Home Loan Bank Act could not even be regarded as a makeshift. It did not, as the Administration predicted, prevent poor and down-trodden mortgagors from losing their properties, and it did not create new funds for real estate financing. It was no wonder, therefore, that even the Administration soon realized the utter futility of this System and recommended broad changes in it.

INCREASE IN NATIONAL BANK NOTE CIRCULATION

To the Home Loan Bank Act was attached the so-called Glass-Borah Amendment, which provided for the increase of national bank notes in circulation. Up to July 22, 1932, when the Home Loan Bank Act was passed, only three issues bearing a coupon rate of 2 per cent had the circulation privilege. On June 30, 1932, the total of these 2 per cent bonds outstanding amounted to $674,625,000. The Glass-Borah Amendment made eligible as security for national bank notes for a period of three years all bonds of the United

States Government bearing interest at 3⅜ per cent or less, those outstanding at the time and those which might be issued during the period. On June 30, 1932, $3,088,813,000 of such bonds were outstanding. Since, however, the amount of national bank notes which an individual national bank might issue was limited to the amount of its paid-in capital, the notes could be increased only to the extent of $1,568,983,000, which was the total paid-up capital on June 30, 1932. But, since the national banks throughout the country had already issued notes to the extent of $652,168,000, the new law made possible an increase of only $916,815,000 in new national bank notes.

The purpose of this provision on the surface is obscure. The Federal Reserve System was established in order to provide the country with a flexible currency. The currency structure of the Reserve banks was sound. The volume of notes outstanding expanded and contracted in accordance with the demands of business. As a matter of fact, when the Federal Reserve Act was passed, provision was made for the issuance of Federal Reserve bank notes for the purpose of eliminating national bank notes entirely. Why, then, the provision to increase the amount of national bank notes outstanding? It was merely a sop to the inflationists, and was so regarded at the time by Senator Glass, the sponsor of the measure in the Senate.

It should be remembered in this connection that the House had passed the so-called Goldsborough Bill, which made it imperative for the Reserve Board to increase prices to the level of 1926. While this bill did not pass the Senate, it was necessary to counteract the activities of some of the most vociferous inflationists. Since the belief still prevailed that the amount of currency needed only to be increased in order to bring about a rise in prices, the Glass-Borah Amendment to the Home Loan Act was passed as a compromise in order to satisfy those who clamored for more currency. As a result of this provision, the amount of national bank notes in circulation increased from $700,890,000 at the end of June, 1932, to $820,497,000 at the end of December, 1932. The new national bank notes brought about merely a decrease in the volume of other types of currency in circulation.

The passage of the Home Loan Act marked the end of the period of "shot-in-the-arm" methods. While they could not bring about a fundamental change in the weakened financial structure of the country, they acted as an opiate; they quieted down temporarily the nerves of the people and offered a splendid opportunity for adopting more fundamental measures. No such basic correctives were taken.

CHAPTER VII.—THE PANIC BEGINS

THE PSEUDO-REVIVAL OF 1932

The threads of the narrative can now be woven together. The month of June, 1932, marked the culmination of the runs on the dollar from abroad. The earmarking of a final $50,000,000 in gold by the Bank of France at the Federal Reserve Bank of New York gave a dramatic finis to the foreign withdrawals.

The Administration's relief measures also became most effective in stemming the bank failure epidemic and the hoarding panic at this time. It is true that, after an initial success, the Reconstruction Finance Corporation and the other "shot-in-the-arm" relief measures seemed to break down early in June with the outbreak of a severe bank failure epidemic in the city of Chicago that quickly affected the surrounding areas. Illinois permits no branch banking at all, so that Chicago had been a chronic "sore-spot" right along. At the beginning of the depression the city and its environs had fully 250 separate banks. By 1932, there were less than 150, and nearly half of these collapsed in June and July of that year. The Insull failure at this time materially helped in the precipitation of a crisis in Chicago.

The Reconstruction Finance Corporation stepped aside for a while, and bank failures rose again to 151 in June and 132 in July. Then the Corporation stepped in decisively in the case of the Central Republic Bank & Trust Company, which General Charles G. Dawes, Chairman of the Reconstruction Corporation, had long headed. After terrific runs, this bank had left some $95,000,000 of deposits. A loan equal to the full amount of these deposits, thus constituting an effective guarantee, was obtained, chiefly from the Reconstruction Corporation. The bank was liquidated without loss to depositors, and for a period thereafter it was assumed definitely by a large section of the public that no large banks would be allowed to fail. Small institutions continued to close, but the total suspensions for the country fell to 85 in August and only 67 in September.

The end of the run on the dollar and of the major bank failure epidemic, coupled with the adjournment of Congress and the successful termination of the Lausanne Conference, created the widespread view that the depression had definitely hit bottom. Accordingly, the rebound started, especially in the speculative markets. The level of stock prices rose fully 100 per cent from the low touched in the first few days of July to the high point of the rally in September and early October. Bonds followed suit. Commodity prices also surged upwards from the June lows, business activity increased, unemployment showed some small abatement—all the conventional earmarks of recovery now made their appearance.

The opinion came to prevail that the country had now weathered its financial crisis and had overcome the financial problems which threatened the maintenance of the gold standard. The dollar once again became the favorite currency throughout the world, selling at a premium in all markets. No wonder, then, that in the political campaign which preceded the elections of November 8 the Administration claimed credit for great accomplishments. Although somewhat overshadowed by political propaganda and by the excitement of the elections, however, the crisis marched on with clock-like precision. The mills of the gods grind slowly, but they grind exceeding small. Every passing day that saw no fundamental measures taken to remedy the inherent weaknesses of the financial structure of the country brought the collapse nearer.

The question is often raised: Why should the banking structure of the United States have collapsed after the various measures adopted by the Administration, and in particular the work of the Reconstruction Finance Corporation, had begun to bear fruit? The answer is not hard to find. The work of the Reconstruction Finance Corporation carried in itself the germ of the later collapse. As was stated before, all loans made by the Reconstruction Finance Corporation had to be adequately secured, so that the best assets of a number of banks were hypothecated, leaving little available to meet any further demands by depositors. A series of circumstances now was to bring out this fundamental weakness.

PUBLICITY FOR R. F. C. LOANS

So long as people did not know which banks were borrowing from the Reconstruction Finance Corporation, the fact that thousands of banks had to have recourse to the latter made little or no impression on depositors. A sudden agitation, however, soon stirred the country into believing that the Reconstruction Finance Corporation was favoring larger institutions, particularly those whose higher officials were closely connected with the Administration. Consequently, the Clerk of the House interpreted the law as requiring him to publish the names of all borrowers. The publication of the names only proved that the Reconstruction Finance Corporation had done what circumstances demanded, that it had made large loans to individual banking institutions because of the disastrous effects that their closing might have produced on smaller banks in certain sections of the country. If the Reconstruction Finance Corporation had not come to the assistance of Mr. Dawes' bank, for example, it would have caused damage and destruction to banks throughout the Middle West.

The disadvantages of publicity were soon apparent. As the names of the borrowing banks appeared in the papers throughout the country, individual depositors of such banks began to withdraw their deposits. A quiet run set in on a number of these institutions. So long as they had collateral available to pledge as security for additional loans from the Reconstruction Finance Corporation, they could obtain new cash to meet the run, but sooner or later either the collateral gave out or the Reconstruction Finance Corporation realized that it was impossible to stem the run, and banks once again began to fail in large numbers. During October, 1932, 103 banks failed, with far-reaching effect. They destroyed again the belief of a large number of people in the United States, revived after the Chicago episode was past that with the Reconstruction Finance Corporation in operation large failures were impossible.

The structure had been shaken, but this was as nothing compared to the earthquake that was to come. Disclosures concerning the causes of the collapse of the Insull organization at this time had a marked adverse effect on the psychology of the American people. The Kreuger & Toll affair had to a considerable extent discredited financial leadership in Wall Street. It revealed that well established and highly respected investment banking houses in the United States had issued bonds of corporations and recommended them as safe investments without adequate check on the financial position of the borrower. The Insull affair revealed some of our great industrial leaders, hitherto regarded by the country as financial wizards, in all their weakness and greed. And with the fall of the idols of gold with feet of clay went billions of dollars of the savings of investors throughout the country.

A NEW HOARDING PANIC

Whatever confidence the people might have had in the permanence of the recovery was shattered by a new series of disturbing events. The Maine elections of October 12 raised a political bugaboo, and the Administration thenceforth encouraged the view that a national Democratic victory would make "grass grow in Wall Street." It also became evident that new taxes had failed to restore the budget to even a semblance of balance. The war debts issue was also appearing on the horizon again with the end of the Hoover one-year moratorium.

The feeling of hopelessness grew; values again declined and cash was all that counted to many. Hoarding in one form or another began to increase again. Government securities were selling at very low yields and interest rates were the lowest in the history of the nation, but bank failures increased just the same. Rumblings through the country about coming banking difficulties became more and more alarming, with one community after another being added to the list of reported "sore spots."

Unable to cope with the situation and unable to obtain new cash with which to keep the banks open, a number of mayors in several of the western states declared banking holidays, either closing the banks in their cities entirely or permitting them to pay out only a small percentage of their deposits. Although Federal banking authorities declared that municipal mayors or other local officials had no power to grant such moratoria, and although the Attorney General of Minnesota actually ruled that municipal moratoria were illegal, the practice continued. It was an ominous foreboding of what was to come.

THE NEVADA MORATORIUM

The first major shock occurred on October 31, when the Lieutenant Governor of Nevada declared a banking holiday for twelve days because of the difficulties of twelve banks with about $17,000,000 of deposits, controlled by George Wingfield. The effect on the State of Nevada of the closing of twelve banks out of a total of twenty-five can easily be imagined. The statement of the Lieutenant Governor in declaring the banking holiday contained the following ominous sentence: "The situation has at last been reached where the conditions can no longer be met by ordinary banking methods without reorganization. It has become necessary to call upon the public to understand the problem and to unite in the plan to save it."

Nevada was the first state to admit that the situation had reached a point where it was beyond the control of managements that had placed the banks in such a pitiable condition. It was the first notice to the public that substantial losses on their deposits would have to be taken. What was the attitude of the other thirteen banks that remained open? Did they endeavor to assist the twelve banks in avoiding a major crash? According to newspaper reports, the other thirteen banks decided not to take advantage of the moratorium, the dispatches stating: "It is possible that they hope thereby to gain business now held by the closed banks." Shades of the Bank of the United States! Had they learned no lesson from New York, where, because of petty intrigues which had prevented the reorganization and the maintenance of a bank with over $200,000,000 in deposits, the other banks were placed in a position where runs on themselves had been either imminent or actually occurred? The similar German experience apparently had no meaning for them either. They merely thought that by closing the Wingfield banks they would be in a position to increase their own deposits. What was the attitude of the Federal authorities? Were not they aware that a bank holiday declared in one state might spread like wild fire throughout the other states?

The first shock had occurred. Depositors in neighboring states became more nervous. Slow but steady withdrawals of bank deposits took place. The two weeks' bank holiday in Nevada passed with no reorganization taking place; another two-week moratorium had to be granted on November 12. These two weeks also passed without any definite action, and at the end of the second period another moratorium, now for three weeks, was announced. The inability of the State and Federal authorities to remedy the situation in Nevada was a clear indication that conditions had gone too far, and that there was no other way to help individual banks or groups of banks in difficulties than by granting moratoria.

The only solution that many economists and bankers could suggest was a national guarantee of bank deposits. It was not enough that the Reconstruction Finance Corporation had poured hundreds of millions of dollars into the weak banks; they wanted the government to underwrite all the losses of banks which should never have been in existence in the first place. They did not think of the fact that such a measure would have a disastrous effect on the credit of the Government, already greatly weakened by continuous staggering deficits. The credit standing of the government was, in fact, the one ray of hope in the entire difficult situation. If the government credit had been ruined, the task of reconstruction would have become all the more difficult. A guarantee, withal, would in no sense give the fundamental correction of our banking structure that was needed urgently.

An examination of the Wingfield group of banks revealed that the depositors would have to take a loss of at least $3,000,000. It is obvious that this news, coupled with the fact that the moratorium was continuously renewed and prolonged, affected adversely the banks in other states. Banking holidays were declared in towns in Illinois, Iowa and in many towns throughout the country. Mayors and other local officials took it upon themselves more than ever to extend banking holidays or to limit the activities of the banks to a point where the claims of their depositors need not be met in full.

The measures adopted by the mayors, however, were no longer sufficient. It became necessary for the states themselves to take cognizance of the collapsing banking structure. Nevada, on October 31, had taken the lead. For a time, it was believed that this would be only an isolated instance and that the banks in the other states would be able to ride out the storm without invoking extraordinary measures. This proved to be a false hope.

The situation had gone too far, and drastic action on the part of state governments became necessary if the banks were to be kept open at all.

THE PANIC GATHERS FORCE

On January 20, 1933, the Iowa General Assembly passed a bill authorizing the State Superintendent of Banking, for a period of one year, to operate any state bank without placing it in receivership. The bill provided that once the management of the bank had been assumed by the Superintendent of Banking, new deposits received had to be segregated from the deposits held at the time application for state management had been made. The new deposits were to be held in trust, and could be withdrawn in full by the depositors. The old deposits and assets were handled according to the rules prescribed by the Superintendent of Banking, presumably for the best interests of depositors and creditors.

This state had finally recognized the fact that, if all the banks which could not meet the demands of their depositors were to be closed, a large number of state banks would soon have to go out of business. The new law enabled the State Superintendent of Banks to keep banks open by allowing them to pay out only a small percentage of the old deposits. While the provision for segregation of new deposits was designed to bring currency back from hoarding, it had an adverse effect on the psychology of depositors in neighboring states. Feeling that sooner or later similar laws would be passed in their own states, they resorted to steady withdrawals so that they could place themselves in the preferred position of new depositors should their banks be subjected to the same legislation. In the East, however, little attention was paid to these measures. With many banks there in a highly liquid position, they felt that nothing that took place in other states could affect them.

Things moved apace. Suddenly, without any warning, the people throughout the United States learned, on February 4, 1933, that the State of Louisiana had declared a public holiday on Saturday, the 4, in commemoration of the severance of diplomatic relations between the United States and the Imperial German Government. The announcement of the Governor of the State of Louisiana is worth quoting:

"Whereas on the nights of February 3 and 4, 1917, Woodrow Wilson, President of the United States, severed diplomatic relations with the Imperial German Government and,

"Whereas more than 16 years have intervened before the American people have turned their eyes back to the lofty ideals of human uplift and new freedom as propounded by Woodrow Wilson . . . and,

"Whereas it is now fitting that due recognition be given by the great State of Louisiana in line with the far-reaching principles enunciated by that illustrious Southerner who sought to break the fetters of mankind throughout the world. . . .

"Now, therefore, I, Oscar Kelly Allen, Governor of the State of Louisiana, do hereby ordain that Saturday, the 4th day of February, 1933 . . . be a holiday throughout the State . . . and I do hereby order that all public business, including schools, banks and other public enterprises be suspended . . . and that the proper ceremonies to commemorate that event be held."

The people not only in Louisiana but throughout the United States could not believe their own eyes. It was delicate irony, not without shrewdness, to declare a holiday on account of the severance of diplomatic relations at a time when the Far East was ablaze with war, when two unofficial wars were raging in South America, and when Europe was again subject to one of the nationalistic waves which in the past had either threatened or destroyed the peace of the world. Here was the great State of Louisiana declaring a state holiday to celebrate the new freedom proposed by Woodrow Wilson. Freedom, when most of Europe and of the South American countries were ruled by dictators!

It did not take long, however, to ascertain the true meaning of the state holiday. One large bank in New Orleans needed respite from its depositors and its obligations, at least for one day, in order to enable it to obtain loans and to arrange its affairs so as to be able to withstand the run of its depositors. The precedent set by Nevada was followed by Louisiana, but the Kingfish of Louisiana, Senator Huey Long, had to resort to clownish means in order to divert the attention of the people from the serious banking situation which confronted the State. "*Panem et Circenses,*" cried the Roman mobs. Unable to give them their bank deposits, the Kingfish gave the people of Louisiana amusement.

The shock of the Louisiana holiday was felt throughout the South and reached as far north as Baltimore. Fortunately, the banks in New Orleans had more foresight than those in Nevada. Loans were obtained wherever possible, and the Hibernia Trust Company on February 6 opened its doors one hour earlier than usual and declared proudly that it was in a position to pay out all deposits. The damage, however, had been done. The feeling that the banking structure of the entire country was collapsing was spreading rapidly everywhere. Interior banks, in order to meet demands of their customers, began to withdraw their deposits from New York City banks, and the latter in turn, in order to meet these demands, were forced to have recourse to the Federal Reserve bank. Currency circulation expanded at an accelerated pace.

It was still believed by many leading bankers in the East, however, that the situation could be localized and that sooner or later quiet would be restored.

Whatever confidence the people might have had in the ability of our legislators to bring us out of the quagmire again was dispelled by the antics of the lame-duck session of Congress and the performances of some of our elected representatives in connection with the Glass Bill. The country was sitting on the edge of a volcano; the financial structure of the country was rocking to its very foundation; business was at a low ebb; the number of unemployed was increasing; throughout the country great efforts were being made to stave off starvation for millions of people—and our legislators in Washington were reading the Bible to prevent a vote on Senator Glass' bank reform measure. Small wonder that people began to feel, "Save himself who can."

THE MICHIGAN BANKS CLOSE

The sense of security of the large commercial banks in the East, based on their extraordinary liquidity, was suddenly jarred by the news that the State of Michigan on February 14, 1933, had declared a banking holiday until February 21, 1933. The time for clownish gestures, for finding an excuse for bank holidays, was gone. Governor William A. Comstock of Michigan declared frankly that, in view of the acute financial emergency existing in the City of Detroit and throughout the State of Michigan, he deemed it necessary in the public interest and, upon the request of the Michigan Bankers' Association and the Detroit Clearing House Association, to declare a state holiday. With one stroke of the pen the bank deposits of the State of Michigan, amounting to approximately $1,500,000,000 and involving about 550 banks, were tied up. The financial resources of one of the greatest industrial states of the Union thus became frozen overnight.

Even before the closing of all the banks in Michigan, there had been frequent rumors about the banks in Detroit. After the closing of the banks there, it became known that the Union Guardian Trust Company, owned by the Guardian Detroit Union group which operated about twenty banks and trust companies in Michigan, had found itself in difficulty due to heavy withdrawals, and needed money in large amounts in order to keep open. On February 13 it became obvious that, unless the Union Guardian Trust Company obtained loans to pay off virtually all its deposits, such as had been granted the Dawes bank in Chicago, it would not be able to open its doors on the following day. It was feared that the closing of the Union Guardian Trust Company would in turn affect all other institutions in the Guardian Detroit Union group, with dire effects on all other banks. The seriousness of the situation could be seen from the fact that the Michigan authorities got in close touch with the United States Treasury, the Federal Reserve Bank, the Reconstruction Finance Corporation and the Secretary of Commerce, who was then in the City of Detroit. All these agencies, combined with the great resources of some of the large automobile manufacturers of Detroit, were not able to provide the millions that would have enabled the Union Guardian Trust Company to pay off its depositors in full.

Immediate aid, however, was granted to the state in a form entirely unexpected. William H. Moran, Chief of the United States Secret Service, declared that he had dispatched 350 secret service operatives throughout Michigan to keep a close watch on scandal-mongers and others who might spread "unfounded rumors" about the banks. What Michigan needed was cash, hard cash, and lots of it, with which to pay frantic depositors, and not secret service operatives to eavesdrop on what the people were saying about their financial institutions which had left them high and dry.

Newspaper stories indicated that a conflict between Henry Ford and Senator Couzens made negotiations for a loan to the Union Guardian Trust Company impossible. While these rumors were later denied, it is very likely that petty jealousies among the various people concerned made it impossible to obtain the necessary funds with which to keep the Union Guardian Trust Company open. The amount involved, considering the total deposits tied up in Michigan, and particularly considering the effect which the closing of all the banks in a state would have on the country as a whole, was comparatively small. Here was another example of the fine *esprit de corps* that had been shown in the case of the Bank of the United States towards the end of 1930, in the case of the German banks in July, 1931, and in the State of Nevada only a few months before.

The shock caused by the Michigan bank holiday was still reverberating throughout the country, when the sub-committee of the Senate Committee on Banking and Currency revealed the activities of Charles E. Mitchell, the Chairman of the National City Bank and its affiliates. This testimony came on top of the Insull investigation, in which Charles G. Dawes, household god of finance for many years, was reputed to have admitted that his bank had violated the spirit of the Illinois bank law when it made loans to the Insull companies to an amount exceeding 15 per cent of its capital and surplus, although he insisted that the procedure was technically within the law. Such revelations of the activities of our first financial leaders, at a time when the eyes of the public were fixed on the banks, were bound to destroy the last vestige of confidence in our financial leadership. Although the congressional investigation proved in many ways highly desirable and useful to the community as well as to the banks, it was ill-timed from this viewpoint.

THE PANIC SPREADS

The closing of the Michigan banks marked the beginning of the final crash. From then on the drama of the collapse rose rapidly to the climax and engulfed state after state. The grand finale was on. Michigan was the last straw that broke the camel's back and set in motion a maddened rush on the part of the depositors for their money. The large financial institutions in the East, which had felt themselves to be in an impregnable position because of their great liquidity, were confronted with a triple run: interior banks were withdrawing their funds as fast as possible; local depositors clamored for cash, gold as well as paper currency; while some of our patriots either sold the dollar short for speculative purposes or transferred their funds to other nations. The only threat to the gold standard in the United States, the enemy from within, was standing before the portals of the Reserve banks, clamoring for gold. People throughout the length and breadth of the nation began to make preparations for the pending collapse. Notes in circulation increased at an alarming rate, while the gold holdings of the central banks decreased rapidly.

The foreign money centers in turn became alarmed, and not without cause. On February 16, Associated Press accounts from Paris stated: "The dollar sank to-day in what bankers described as a demoralized market reflecting French concern over the Michigan banking situation. Dollars opened at 25.43, which was six centimes under yesterday's close and quickly dropped to 25.34." On the other hand, a leading New York financial weekly stated on February 18: "As to the banking moratorium in Michigan, that obviously is a serious affair, not to be treated lightly, and yet furnishing occasion for satisfaction in that it appears to have been handled with consummate skill and that it seems possible to say that the worst of the trouble now lies behind, with good reasons for thinking that there will be an early return to the normal. Help has come from every side, as is always the case when financial difficulties are encountered in this country."

However, the precious days of the Michigan bank holiday were permitted to pass one by one without bringing a solution to the problem. With the eyes of the whole nation turned toward the scene of one of the greatest banking calamities in history, the giants of finance and the captains of industry, in utter disregard of the depositors' interests and of the impending collapse of the nation's banking structure, refused to agree on an equitable solution in spite of all the pleadings, persuasion and pressure of state and federal officials and all the proffered financial assistance.

The conflagration spread! State after state adopted measures authorizing the restriction of deposit withdrawals in order to preserve their assets and to provide equal protection to depositors. On February 21, even before the Michigan bank holiday had come to an end, Governor Moore of New Jersey signed a bill providing that banks could keep new deposits separated from old accounts, and giving the banking officials the power to extend for 90 days or more the notice required on withdrawals of time deposits. The Banking Commissioner was also permitted to postpone payment of any proportion of demand accounts. The panic had spread from the Middle West and had at last reached the East. It was standing before the doors of New York.

Michigan could not find a solution to the bank problems of Detroit. When the moratorium expired, the banks were allowed to pay out only small amounts for necessities. The formula to cure the disease and to restore confidence had not been found. The panic grew, and on Saturday, February 25, the State of Maryland was forced to declare a holiday and other states followed in rapid succession. The panic was on!

CHAPTER VIII.—THE COLLAPSE IS COMPLETE

STATE MORATORIA

The Michigan bank holiday started the banking pânic—the Maryland moratorium clinched it. All over the country bankers, business men and government officials had been hoping against hope that the Detroit fiasco could be localized, and that the old banking order could be maintained for at least a while longer. The collapse in Maryland was the last straw, and popular confidence broke down completely under it.

Nevertheless, over the week-end attempts were still being made to patch things up. The Detroit bankers, distraught after continuous conferences through the previous week, finally agreed to turn their banks over to Henry Ford, who agreed to reorganize them as sole stockholder and release 35 per cent of the deposits. Under this plan, he would become virtual banking dictator of the state on the basis of a capital investment of $8,250,000. In addition, $54,000,000 was to be provided by the Reconstruction Finance Corporation and $20,000,-000 by New York bankers, on the security of sound assets. At the same time, the press announced that Charles E. Mitchell had resigned from the management of the National City Bank and its affiliates, a step which served to clarify the situation in New York City. Any hope that these events would suffice to maintain the *status quo* was quickly dispelled, however. When business opened on Monday, February 27, banks all over Ohio and Indiana announced restrictions on withdrawals, while long lines of depositors were forming outside financial institutions all over the country. The public had decided to turn its funds into the form of cash.

Bankers are individualists, and this characteristic was especially marked as the panic gathered force. Each thought primarily of his ability to keep his own institution open, regardless of the general situation. The true state of affairs was well illustrated in Ohio, where a number of the weaker banks, notably several in Cleveland, had been urging Governor White over the week-end to have a state-wide moratorium declared similar to that already announced in Michigan and Maryland. The Cincinnati banks, on the other hand, relatively strong owing to the fact that this city had avoided a real estate boom during the preceding prosperity period and boasted conservative banking management, opposed such a move. They claimed they could stay open and meant to do so.

Governor White thereupon hurried through the legislature a bill permitting banks to restrict withdrawals of deposits by authority of the State Banking Commissioner, and on Monday morning every Clearing House bank in Cleveland except the National City Bank restricted withdrawals to 5 per cent. Immediately, depositors in Cleveland banks who had funds elsewhere began to withdraw them to obtain needed cash, while fears of restrictions caused a run on the open banks all over the state. By the very next morning, the Cincinnati Clearing House banks themselves were forced to announce restrictions on withdrawals to 5 per cent of deposits, although the First National Bank did not follow suit and remained open.

The rapid deterioration of the Ohio situation and the virtual shutdown of Indiana banks was accompanied on Tuesday by terrific runs all over the country. The public, which had displayed heroic stoicism during nearly three years of bank failures, was finally aroused. No longer were individual banks failing "like the leaves in Vallombrosa," as Senator Carter Glass had described it. The collapse was more nearly like a Presidential political convention. The banks were joining the ranks of closed institutions by states.

At the opening of business Wednesday morning, March 1, banks in Alabama, California, Idaho, Kentucky, Louisiana, Mississippi and Tennessee all had bank holidays. While several individual institutions remained open in varying degrees in these states, business was paralyzed. The country was gradually moving back a long period of decades as currency was replacing bank checks as the chief medium of exchange. Where the banks remained open, the public in self-defense rushed to the tellers' windows to get cash before it was too late. Many, including both the sophisticated and the scared, sought to transform both currency and bank deposits into gold, fearing an early abandonment of the gold standard.

The first three days of March witnessed the height of the banking panic. A total of $732,000,000 in money was taken out of the banks that stayed open in the week ended March 1, chiefly in the last two days of the week. During the following two days, fully $818,000,000 in money was drawn out of the banks. Since the commercial banks of the country, numbering about 16,500 at the time, possessed approximately $28,000,000,000 of deposits, the experience of the first three days of March indicated that withdrawals were going on at the rate of about 10 per cent weekly.

AN OLD-FASHIONED MONEY PANIC

Through it all, the New York and Chicago banks, as well as numerous institutions in other communities throughout the country, remained open. The large Wall Street banks generally enjoyed a high degree of liquidity—that is, they had a large proportion of their deposits with the Federal Reserve Banks, invested in government bonds, bankers' acceptances, call loans on stock exchange collateral, etc. But the New York institutions, despite the existence of the Federal Reserve banks, were still bankers' banks, in large measure, as had been the case in the period before the Reserve System was established. The New York City reporting member banks of the Federal Reserve System, comprising virtually all the Wall Street banks, held $1,418,000,000 in out-of-town bank deposits on February 14, as shown by their item of "due to banks." A fortnight later, this had shrunk by fully $520,000,000, and the shrinkage continued. Out-of-town corporations also withdrew freely from their city depositories in order to meet payments in states where the banks were closed. New York thus had to withstand a twofold run, heavy withdrawals from out-of-town banks and corporations going on at the very time that their local depositors were asking that their deposits be turned into cash on a large scale.

The New York banks in turn looked to their Federal Reserve bank for aid. They sold bankers' acceptances which were absorbed freely by the Federal Reserve, and they rediscounted eligible paper. Thus, the burden of providing cash to meet the enormous deposit withdrawals finally rested squarely on the Federal Reserve.

An old-fashioned money panic was on. People wanted to turn their bank deposits into cash. The schoolbooks had taught for years that in such a crisis the Federal Reserve banks would provide all the currency needed, and that the panic would thus prove little more than a ripple on the smooth surface of Reserve bank operation. But the schoolbooks were shown to be wrong.

The Federal Reserve System was designed to provide a "flexible currency," one that would expand and contract with the needs of trade. But now a currency was needed that was flexible in the sense of being capable of expansion to replace bank deposits to an indefinite extent. Before the panic, there were outstanding approximately $28,000,000,000 of commercial banking deposits and $5,500,000,000 of paper and metallic money in circulation throughout the country. As the panic developed, the public demanded that a large part of the $28,000,000,000 of commercial bank deposits, and in addition a good part of the $11,000,000,000 of savings bank deposits, be turned into cash. On March 3, when the peak of monetary circulation had been reached, more than $7,500,000,000 of metallic and paper money were actually outstanding.

The Federal Reserve banks could not meet this type of demand for flexibility. Each Federal Reserve note, since the passage of the Glass-Steagall bill, required a reserve of 40 per cent in gold and 60 per cent in commercial paper or government securities. The 40 per cent gold cover clause thus proved the neck of the bottle, and was the chief factor which finally forced a general closing down of the banks.

THE LOSS OF GOLD

At the very time that the Reserve banks' need for gold was rising sharply in order to provide the 40 per cent gold cover on notes, their gold stocks were being slowly whittled down. There were two main leaks through which gold was lost. One was the export of the metal or its earmarking for foreign account, the latter operation being the equivalent to exports in that it cut gold stocks so far as this country was concerned. For the week ended March 1, a loss of $116,000,000 in gold was registered on this account. In the second place, people were turning currency into gold, mostly through presenting Federal Reserve notes for exchange into gold at the gold room of the Federal Reserve bank of New York. As the panic week progressed, long lines formed to exchange ever larger amounts of currency for gold there, until finally the metal was being carried away in large boxes and suitcases loaded on trucks. For the week ended March 1, the Federal Reserve banks lost an additional $100,000,000 in gold to domestic hoarders.

The second and third days of March witnessed the further loss of $108,000,000 of gold through exports and earmarkings, mainly the latter, and $101,000,000 of the yellow metal taken by domestic hoarders. For the nine days ended March 3, therefore, $425,000,000 of gold left the Reserve banks.

The metal earmarked for foreign account represented chiefly the flight of capital from this country, rather than withdrawals of foreign balances. The latter had long ago been reduced to relatively small proportions by the runs on the dollar described in Chapter V above. In addition, there was a huge short interest in the dollar built up by sales of dollars by foreigners abroad for future delivery, or purchases of foreign exchange here on 30, 60, or 90 days contracts. The extent to which Americans were going short of the dollar here was shown by the fact that sterling drafts for delivery in 90 days sold at a 10 cent premium above the prevailing "spot" rate covering immediate deliveries of British exchange.

The reason why the flight from the dollar became largely a shift from dollars to sterling may be explained by the fact that the British currency, being divorced from the gold standard, had become highly volatile. It became evident that a huge speculative demand for sterling was arising, not only in this country, but also in France and elsewhere on the continent where the gold standard seemed threatened. It was anticipated that a sharp rise in the pound would occur merely because of the huge demand which developed. The speculators reasoned that by buying pounds they could expect to profit in one of two ways—either by a rise in the pound or a drop in the dollar through abandonment of the gold standard here.

The quotation of the British pound was affected in large measure, however, by the operation of the Equalization Fund of £150,000,000 set up by Act of Parliament and operated by the British exchequer as a means of preventing major fluctuations. When the pound was weak, the Equalization Fund bought, and when it was strong it sold pounds. The run on the dollar created a huge demand for pounds sterling which the Equalization Fund met by selling pounds, thus preventing an artificial rise in its quotation. The Equalization Fund came to be possessed of quite large sums in dollars in this way. As a reasonable precaution against a fall in the dollar through abandonment of the gold standard, these dollar balances were converted by the Bank of England into earmarked gold here. The huge earmarkings of gold thus represented chiefly acquisition of the yellow metal by the British Equalization Fund in its battle to keep the pound from being forced upward. The speculators failed to dislodge the Equalization Fund from the market. The expected profit from a rise in the pound did not materialize, therefore, but the more persistent of the speculators did profit from the final abandonment of the gold standard by the United States on April 15, 1933.

Estimates of the volume of dollar funds temporarily transferred abroad during the banking panic, and the amount of forward exchange transactions engaged in for speculative purposes, ranged up to $500,000,000 and even $700,000,000 at the time.

THE NEW YORK BANKS SUSPEND

Under the dual pressure of currency withdrawals and gold losses, the Federal Reserve banks were soon at the end of their resources. The pressure centered on the Federal Reserve bank of New York, which was forced to a number of extraordinary expedients, including borrowings from other Federal Reserve banks, to obtain gold as cover for additional issues of Federal Reserve notes. The Federal Reserve agent, the Treasury's chief representative in each Reserve bank, could issue Federal Reserve notes to the bank only as the required gold and other cover was put up with him as collateral, and despite all the expedients taken, at the close of business, March 3, the margin of free gold was small or nil in most of the Reserve banks.

On Friday afternoon, the day before Inauguration, the New York banks had had their worst runs. Nevertheless, relying upon their "liquidity," or ability to shift their assets to the Federal Reserve banks in exchange for circulating notes, many of them insisted upon being allowed to stay open. Commendable though this desire to stay open for business was, it impeded efforts to handle the situation on a proper scale and with a view to an ultimate solution. The deterioration of the country's banking position had proceeded to the point where the situation had to be handled on a national scale and with drastic measures. However, the fact that the Federal Reserve bank of New York was not in position to issue notes much longer, with its ratio of gold reserve to deposit and note liabilities dropping below 40 per cent, and the indicated demand for currency for the morrow greater than ever, was the deciding factor in the situation.

The dramatic climax occurred at the home of Governor Lehman of New York in the early morning of Inauguration Day. After continuous conferences among the Clearing House banks and at the Federal Reserve banks, the financial leaders of the city met at the Governor's home uptown late at night and outlined the situation. At this meeting, the predicament of the Federal Reserve bank of New York, caused by the dual strain of gold and currency withdrawals on a huge scale to provide money for a whole country in which the banks were progressively closing by state action, was fully aired. The Governor, who that afternoon had stated that he had not been asked for a bank holiday and expected none, issued at 4.20 A. M. his historic proclamation declaring a two-day general banking holiday for the State of New York. The Chicago banks and the security and commodity exchanges of the country closed down at the same time to prevent panic liquidation, and the collapse was all but complete.

President Roosevelt's inauguration was marked by an event that had never transpired before to celebrate the induction of a new Administration. The banks of the country were closed on that fateful Saturday, but not in joy or celebration. Almost alone, the banks of Pittsburgh, dominated by the great and powerful Mellon institutions there, did not close their doors. The institutions controlled by the family of President Hoover's Secretary of the Treasury were open while Mr. Hoover's successor was being inducted into office.

THE PRESIDENT'S PROCLAMATION

The first problem thus facing the new President was a financial collapse of perhaps unparalleled severity. Mr. Roosevelt acted to confirm a *fait accompli* with a proclamation at midnight of March 5, shutting down the financial institutions of the country for a four-day period under a law unearthed from the archives of government after some 15 years of disuse—the Trading with the Enemy Act. This dust-covered statute, not repealed because of legislative carelessness, was held to be still in force. Lawyers have since questioned seriously the constitutionality of the whole procedure, but the speed with which events followed gave neither time nor opportunity for questioning the President's doings by action in the courts. The President also suspended the gold standard by prohibition of gold exports, foreign exchange dealings, redemption of notes into gold and hoarding of gold.

In subsequent discussions, especially in the partisan press, the closing of the banks has been hailed as a great achievement of the Democratic party. It would be a very doubtful claim to distinction for any Administration. The closing of the banks in this country, like the abandonment of the pound sterling in Great Britain, may have been inevitable in the light of subsequent events, but it was a disaster of the first magnitude just the same. It would have been far better if the crisis could have been avoided, but the panic precipitated by the mishandling of the Michigan situation occurred during a virtual political interregnum that preceded the inauguration of President Roosevelt. The conditions which made the crisis inevitable were of long standing, but the failure in 1932 of both a Republican Administration and a Congress very largely Democratic to take decisive action to forestall the collapse makes the record of both parties far from complimentary. The President also wisely called the new Congress into special session for Thursday at noon, thus giving himself and his advisers a few days' time in which to devise measures for reopening the banks.

THE SCRIP IDEA

The week of the bank holiday will long be remembered by Americans of this generation as one of suspended animation. People lived on whatever cash they had on hand or could borrow. Small hoards were shared by many. Regular business, already severely depressed, was threatened by wholesale shutdowns due to inability to pay for materials and labor. It was evident that unless the financial machinery of the country were again placed in working order, a major catastrophe threatened. Since the Reserve banks could not meet the demand for currency, efforts were launched immediately to devise an emergency medium of exchange.

To most people, the outstanding issue of the day as detailed in the newspapers of the panic week was whether or not scrip should be issued. During past panics, it was argued, scrip had been issued by Clearing houses. They should do the same now, it was said. Bankers, government officials, Administration advisers urged its use. Clearing houses were to take over sound assets of banks and issue their scrip in exchange, so that a new currency divorced from gold and secured by Clearing house obligations based on sound banking assets could be created. In this way, the commercial banks would be able to overcome the handicap of the virtual breakdown of the Federal Reserve banks caused by the lack of a gold reserve, and they could then reopen at least in part.

The scrip issued in 1907 and other past panics was utilized to settle balances between banks at a time that a money shortage prevailed, since in these earlier days banks regularly settled net balances due each other in money. But, with the establishment of the Federal Reserve System, the banks settled balances among themselves by drawing on their deposits with the Federal Reserve, which they could replenish through rediscounts. Conditions were thus entirely different from those prevailing in these earlier panics, for the Reserve banks could readily perform the functions which the use of scrip had accomplished on those occasions. Unfortunately, a number of bankers and economists who lived through the 1907 period had forgotten that much water had flowed over the dam since, and that the need of the moment—circulating media and not emergency currency to settle bankers' balances—could not be met by devising a new-fangled and unknown type of currency which would further excite suspicions of a public already gravely disillusioned as to the stability of the nation's financial mechanism.

In a few communities like Philadelphia scrip in small amounts was actually issued. In New York, the plants of the American Bank Note Co. ran day and night for a while printing scrip that was never to see the light of day. It had been pointed out by

.M

Aristophanes in the days of Ancient Greece, and by other writers since, that "cheaper money drives out the dear," an adage known to economists as Gresham's law, after Elizabeth's chancellor of the exchequer who had reached the same conclusion. The scrip advocates had overlooked this simple rule. They had failed to recognize the obvious fact that if each community would issue its own scrip, the cities known to have the weaker banks would very soon find their scrip discriminated against. Gradually, a market would be established for scrip of different cities at varying quotations, with a likely resulting further shock to popular confidence that might take years to overcome. Fortunately, the Administration decided after a few days to abandon the scrip idea, and to provide additional currency by utilization of the Federal Reserve banks instead.

In the meanwhile, in view of the nation-wide outcry for funds to carry on ordinary trade, the Secretary of the Treasury issued a series of regulations authorizing withdrawals from the banks, despite the Presidential holiday, for payroll purposes, financing the transportation of foodstuffs, etc. But the regulations were drawn so loosely and inexpertly that enormous confusion resulted. However, limited withdrawals where allowed tended to alleviate the situation somewhat. In retrospect, it is evident that somewhat less rigid of these restrictions, as was done during the German bank holiday of 1931 when depositors could freely withdraw 5 per cent of their deposits, would have alleviated the crushing burden of the moratorium on individuals and on business.

On Thursday, March 9, the special session of the new Congress was to meet at noon. The entire country, the whole world, in fact, centered its attention on this momentous gathering of the national legislature. How and when would the banks reopen, and what would it do as regards the future of the nation's currency? The first question was given an immediate and decisive answer, as the next chapter will show.

CHAPTER IX.—THE BANKS ARE REOPENED

THE COUNTRY AT THE CROSSROADS

FEW Administrations indeed in this country have faced such difficult and delicate problems during the first week of their existence as did that of Franklin D. Roosevelt. The parallel with Lincoln's inauguration immediately suggests itself. Then, disunion and civil war faced the country as the President took office. President Roosevelt faced a nation-wide financial collapse of the first magnitude. In both cases the elected representatives of the people rose to the occasion and took decisive action when faced with the gravest problems. It remains to be seen, however, whether our banking problem can be solved as fundamentally and permanently by Roosevelt as were the slavery and states rights questions by Lincoln seventy years earlier.

President Roosevelt and his new secretary of the Treasury, William H. Woodin, locomotive builder and musician, both smiling, suave and outwardly unruffled, were the enigmas in a baffling situation that faced the country early in March, 1933. While the bankers were conferring feverishly on various and sundry temporary expedients to permit the business of the country to continue from day to day, what were the heads of the newly inducted Administration doing? Would they permit the situation to drift further, or had they devised a plan which would permit the banks to reopen without delay and confidence to be restored? Would they accede to the powerful demands made both within and without the Democratic party for a law guaranteeing bank deposits, which would shift the burden of banking deflation from depositors and stockholders of the banks to the government and thus jeopardize Federal finances and the credit of the United States? Or would they be satisfied with a mere liberalization of the rules governing the operation of the Reconstruction Finance Corporation, so as to syphon funds of the Federal government into the banks through poorly secured loans from that source, in the manner of the Hoover Administration? Would any permanent reform of our banking law be attempted at the same time that emergency relief was administered?

All these questions as to banking policy begged for an answer during those fateful March days, while all the world wondered. Inextricably intertwined with the Administration's decisions on emergency banking legislation, also, would be its decision as to currency policy, and notably the retention of the gold standard and sound money. President Roosevelt, in his inaugural address, said he favored an "adequate but sound currency." These words, cabled round the world, immediately were interpreted by many as signifying that he favored a currency perhaps more adequate than sound—that he might desire a permanent abandonment of the gold standard or a devaluation of the gold content of the dollar. This view had been heightened by the gold export embargo and orders against internal hoarding of gold which had accompanied the President's proclamation of March 5 closing the banks of the country.

THE NEW LEGISLATION

It would be more than the truth to say that the new Administration and its advisers went to work immediately to draft legislation to carry out decisions they were agreed upon from the first. The major alternative was one between inflation and deflation. Should the gold export embargo caused by the banking crisis be utilized to devalue the dollar and raise prices through monetary manipulation, or should the unsound banks be reorganized or permanently closed, with consequent wiping out of billions of bank deposits and intensification of deflation in our economic structure?

The Roosevelt Administration decided to leave the currency question open at the time, both because of divisions of counsel as to the best course to follow, and a desire to regain large amounts of gold held by hoarders. Only the tasks of reopening of the banks, and the taking of steps to make a repetition of the panic impossible, were presented to the new Congress on the first day it was called in special session, March 9. There is good reason to believe that during its first two or three days in office, as the work of drafting the new bills started, there was widespread division of counsel within the Administration. A number of its advisers were known sympathizers with inflationary schemes. On Wednesday, March 8, however, it became evident that banking relief would not involve immediate monetary experimentation. First came the announcement that the scrip idea, favored by the inflationists, had been happily dropped, and that instead the Federal Reserve System would be given authority to provide all the currency that might be needed. It was to be not only adequate but also sound. As subsequent events proved, the mere provision for the issue of the new currency, along with the other measures taken at the time was enough to stem the demand for it, and start conditions back to normal.

THE PRESIDENT'S MESSAGE

When Congress convened on Thursday, March 9, therefore, the President sent it a brief, concise message which outlined his unequivocal choice of policy with classic simplicity. Fears of inflation, of bank deposit guarantees, of unlimited Reconstruction Finance Corporation loans, were set at rest for the moment. It was wisely concluded that, pending the return of normal banking conditions, no monetary steps should be taken which would add to popular uneasiness and panic. The President said:

TO THE SENATE AND HOUSE OF REPRESENTATIVES:

On March 3 banking operations in the United States ceased. To review at this time the causes of this failure of our banking system is unnecessary. Suffice it to say that the government has been compelled to step in for the protection of depositors and the business of the nation.

Our first task is to reopen all sound banks. This is an essential preliminary to subsequent legislation directed against speculation with the funds of depositors and other violation of positions of trust.

In order that the first objective—the opening of banks for the resumption of business—may be accomplished, I ask of the Congress the immediate enactment of legislation giving to the executive branch of the government control over banks for the protection of depositors; authority forthwith to open such banks as have already been ascertained to be in sound condition, and other such banks as rapidly as possible; and authority to reorganize and reopen such banks as may be found to require reorganization to put them on a sound basis.

I ask amendments to the Federal Reserve Act to provide for such additional currency, adequately secured, as it may become necessary to issue to meet all demands for currency and at the same time to achieve this end without increasing the unsecured indebtedness of the government of the United States. . . .

In the short space of five days it is impossible for us to formulate completed measures to prevent the recurrence of the evils of the past. This does not and should not, however, justify any delay in accomplishing this first step.

At an early moment I shall request of the Congress two other measures which I regard as of immediate urgency. With action taken thereon we can proceed to the consideration of a rounded program of national restoration.

FRANKLIN D. ROOSEVELT.

The White House, March 9, 1933.

The President's message thus pointed a definite road out of the crisis, and gave an appearance of extreme conservatism. Wall Street bankers rubbed their eyes. The President, despite his reputed radicalism, acted like one of themselves.

The financiers were to be deeply disappointed on this score before long.

Only the "sound banks" would open, the President announced, and any new currency desired by owners of bank deposits could be obtained only by utilization of the safeguarded facilities of the Federal Reserve System, as liberalized to meet the emergency. He also stated, and this was a source of disappointment to many, that more fundamental measures to correct the banking evils from which the country had suffered so much would be delayed. Perhaps it was wise, to assure the instantaneous support of Congress for the pressing emergency bills, that more controversial permanent measures were held back. But past experience had shown that the passing of an emergency only serves to give the forces that had long opposed necessary basic reforms the time to rally and reform their ranks, thus dealing the cause of lasting correction of the banking troubles of the country a new serious blow. Had the Administration agreed within itself on a bank reform program, Congress, scared and cowed as was the national legislature at that moment of crisis, would surely have passed quickly a far more comprehensive reform measure at the same time.

Immediately after the reading of the President's message, the legislation drafted by the Administration with the aid of Congressional leaders was presented in Congress. Within the record time of 7½ hours, it had been enacted into law, with very few dissenting voices heard. The contents of the new legislation may be summarized as follows:

TITLE ONE

The revolutionary steps taken by the President and the Secretary of the Treasury under the Trading with the Enemy Act were confirmed by Congress. The special powers were continued, to make Administrative approval necessary for the reopening of banks. Special penalties were attached to the hoarding of gold and unlicensed transactions in foreign exchange.

TITLE TWO

The Comptroller of the Currency was authorized to appoint conservators for any national bank where he regarded this step necessary to conserve the bank's assets, replacing the old type of bank closing. The conservator could operate the bank under needed safeguards, thus giving communities in which unsound banks were found some kind of banking service. Speedy reorganization of such banks could be accomplished by approval of 75 per cent of the deposits and, where the equity of the stock had not been wiped out as revealed by an audit of the assets, two-thirds of the capital stock.

TITLE THREE

The reorganization of weak banks was facilitated by authorizing the issuance of non-assessable preferred stock in such cases. Such preferred shares could be issued to depositors or sold to the Reconstruction Finance Corporation.

TITLE FOUR

Federal Reserve bank notes, authorized under the original Federal Reserve Act, were revived and their use vastly extended. These notes, redeemable not in gold but in "lawful money," could be issued up to 100 per cent against government bonds and up to 90 per cent against commercial paper and bankers' acceptances deposited as security. For a maximum two-year period, Reserve banks were to make advances on any acceptable assets of member banks to furnish them with such Federal Reserve bank notes as they were needed. Individuals and corporations, also, were authorized to borrow on their own promissory notes secured by government bonds to obtain needed bank notes, a precaution for the benefit of areas where banking facilities might disappear entirely under the new dispensation.

The new banking bill assured the successful immediate reopening of banks by two fundamental devices:

1. The note-creating ability of the Federal Reserve banks was restored by authorizing them to issue Federal Reserve bank notes, secured by government bonds and other assets, without gold cover. This removed any significant limitations on the manufacture of currency if the public insisted upon proceeding with its effort to turn its bank deposits generally into currency, an effort that had been arrested only by the banking holiday.

2. Member banks were given virtually unlimited access to the Federal Reserve banks for an emergency period, to obtain needed notes should withdrawals of cash continue after the banks were reopened.

These two measures made it possible theoretically for depositors to turn the larger part of their bank deposits into Federal Reserve bank notes. When the banks reopened after the termination of the holiday, however, currency immediately began to flow back to them. The ability to get currency, plus the other steps taken to restore confidence, was enough to kill the desire for it. Instead, a wave of patriotic sentiment and renewed hope spread over the country, and gold and currency flowed back to the banks.

The new law was so broadly drawn that its results were necessarily largely dependent on the manner in which it would be administered. The President, following its enactment, issued a new proclamation extending the bank holiday indefinitely. Thereafter he announced a policy of gradually reopening only the "sound banks" by official authorization as he had promised in his message to Congress. The Secretary of the Treasury was to give authority to Federal Reserve member banks to reopen, while state authorities were granted jurisdiction over the reopening of other financial institutions.

THE BANKS RESUME

The delicate operation of reopening the banks was accomplished with speed and dispatch. Individual institutions filled out form applications for the privilege to reopen, which were then filed with the respective Federal Reserve banks in the case of member institutions and with the proper state authorities for non-members. These authorities, from previous examinations and from further information presented to them by the bank's management, or their own examiners, acted upon the applications. In a number of instances, reopening was authorized several days late, but the great bulk of the banks given the privilege of reopening without reorganization resumed business on schedule. On March 31, Secretary Woodin announced that 365 national banks, with deposits of $350,000,000 had reopened belatedly after they had been reorganized or otherwise strengthened.

The procedure covered a period of three days. On Monday, March 13, institutions in the twelve Federal Reserve cities were reopened. On the following day, banks resumed in cities where recognized clearing houses existed, about 250 in all. On Wednesday, March 15, banks elsewhere were reopened. During this three-day period, more than 12,000 out of the 17,000 odd commercial banking institutions that had been open when the Michigan bank holiday precipitated the crisis had resumed. Of the 5,200 unlicensed banks, 1,141 were under national charter, 166 were state-chartered member banks and 3,900 were state non-member banks.

While most of the casualties were found among the smaller institutions, several banks of major size were included also. In New York City, the Harriman National Bank & Trust Company, a member of the New York Clearing House remained closed when widespread falsification of its books was discovered. For the first time in its eighty years of history, a member of the New York Clearing House had failed!

Detroit, Cleveland, Baltimore and New Orleans were the hardest hit among the large cities, with important institutions kept closed in each instance. In all, it was subsequently reported, there were $1,000,000,000 of deposits in the national banks and $3,000,000,000 in the state banks that did not reopen immediately.

The standards applied by the Secretary of the Treasury in determining which were sound among member banks of the Federal Reserve System, and by the state authorities in doing the same for non-member institutions, were not overly strict. The sweeping declines in asset values generated by three years of deflation, it was felt, made a broad interpretation of the term "sound" imperative. Furthermore, the greatly broadened rediscount privileges made such liberality permissible. The fact that a few banks that were reopened reclosed within the next few weeks clearly indicated that in such instances the reopenings were based upon hopes of a heavy return flow of deposits, and where this did not materialize directors preferred to reorganize banks under the new procedure laid down by the Act.

The Roosevelt banking legislation left the banks to some extent on a sounder basis than they had been before the Michigan holiday, to the extent that more than 3,000 weak institutions reopened under conservators, or did not reopen at all. It ended the need for further banking holidays, through provision of the new currency and through broadening of the rediscount privileges. The easy access granted banks to the Federal Reserve System was enormously extended, furthermore, by the passage by Congress before the end of March of the Robinson-

Steagall Bill, which permitted non-member banks to enjoy for a period of one year the rediscount privilege, for the first time in the history of the Federal Reserve System. These banks had first to deposit funds with the Reserve banks equal to the reserves required of member banks. Naturally, the new law opened up the possibility that the Reserve banks might gradually become loaded as a result with assets of second or worse grade, a possibility that Senator Carter Glass constantly warned against while the new legislation was being debated.

As a result of the banking holiday and the consequent widespread tendency to face facts rather than to ignore them by temporary makeshifts pending a return of prosperity, other types of financial institutions also readjusted their affairs after the banks reopened. The guaranteed mortgage companies in New York City, which had guaranteed $3,000,000,000 of such issues, were placed by the state authorities under restrictions which virtually suspended their guarantees, throwing holders of these obligations back on the underlying mortgage securities. Insurance companies were for a very short time restricted from paying dividends and other benefits in varying degree, pending the writing down of losses they had suffered on their assets. The dividend prohibition on life insurance companies, however, was rescinded within a few days.

REOPENING CLOSED BANKS

During the subsequent months, the government sought to have these closed banks reopened as rapidly as possible after a reorganization which involved the raising of new capital from private and governmental sources. Usually, depositors or others in the community were asked to subscribe to the capital stock of each reorganized institution, and the Reconstruction Finance Corporation made an equal subscription to the preferred stock. To a small extent, local banks were merged in connection with such reorganizations, but in the main no advantage was taken of the crisis to modify the unit banking system of the country which had done so much mischief in the preceding years. The Administration sought to reopen banks as fast as possible in connection with its effort to stimulate an immediate business recovery, giving little attention to any permanent reform of the banking structure in doing so.

By June 29, most of the banks that were easy to reorganize had been licensed. The situation at that time, more than three months after the crisis, may be summarized as on page 181.

It will thus be seen that more than 3,000 banks with almost $2,500,000,000 of deposits remained unlicensed by that date.

The fact that so many individual institutions

remained closed after the Bank Holiday caused deep resentment in the communities affected, and there was persistent pressure from political representatives of these areas for more liberal aid to such institutions. This agitation culminated in October, 1933, in the setting up of a special department of the Reconstruction Finance Corporation under the Deposit Liquidation

	Number of Commercial Banks		Volume of Deposits (000,000 omitted)	
	Open Before Holiday	Unlicensed June 28, 1933	Before Holiday	In Unlicensed Banks, June 28, 1933
			$	$
National	5,886	987	17,902	1,113
State Member ..	820	117	9,974	311
State Non-Member	10,184	2,016	6,143	1,071
Total ..	16,980	3,120	$34,019	$2,495

Board, the avowed purpose of which was to free at least half of the deposits of the closed banks through government advances, to be repaid out of the liquidation of their assets.

The banks that remained unopened by that date were to a large degree those whose assets were very severely impaired, so that heavy losses had to be taken if any substantial repayments were to be assured depositors by the government. The Administration, despite repeated pressure and seeming pliancy, did not choose to take over the losses of these institutions in the way that the German government had taken over banking losses after the 1931 banking crisis in that country. Also, the incidence of deposit guarantee legislation on January 1, 1934, made it necessary to proceed carefully in further reopening of banks, since reorganized institutions of inadequate strength might have to be closed again. Accordingly, depositors of many banks closed by the March panic had to wait for a long time for the payment of even a moderate fraction of their deposits.

CONFIDENCE IS RESTORED

The speedy passage of the new banking legislation, the successful reopening of the great majority of the banks of the country and the impression which gained ground that the Administration would retain the gold standard brought about an immediate revival of popular confidence. The volume of money in circulation during the ten days following the initial reopening of the banks dropped by $930,000,000 of which $509,000,000 represented the return of gold and gold certificates by hoarders who felt reassured or were frightened into returning the yellow metal in exchange for currency by the penalties on such hoarding provided in the law.

Imposition of foreign exchange restrictions,

with Fred I. Kent, director of the Bankers Trust Co. and President of the Council of New York University, veteran of wartime exchange control, in the post of Foreign Exchange Administrator, helped to maintain dollar exchange quotations during this period. Through the drawing up of a set of regulations which nominally limited sales of foreign exchange by the banks in the main to bona fide trade needs, thus compelling dollar shorts to cover as their future contracts expired and they could not replace them with new forward commitments, the demand for dollars through the readjustment period offset further speculative pressure.

The President's banking laws did not achieve any permanent reform of the banking structure, however. The dual measures regarded as most important for a permanent solution of our banking problems—widespread branch banking and unification of the banking system under national charters—had not been accomplished. In fact, by giving state member banks temporary access to the Federal Reserve System, the continued existence of numerous such institutions was assured. Thus, the banking holiday and its immediate aftermath brought no permanent or lasting results as far as commercial banking went. This task, the most important because its results would be most lasting, remained to be done.

CHAPTER X.—THE "NEW DEAL"

THE ROOSEVELT PROGRAM

FOLLOWING the reopening of the banks at the end of the Holiday, the Administration turned its attention to the correction of the basic economic difficulties which had caused the banking structure of the country to collapse. Banking legislation proper played a secondary role in this program, although the Glass-Steagall Act as finally passed on June 16, 1933, contained a revolutionary deposit guarantee scheme which will be taken up later in this chapter.

The program for a managed recovery, designed to end the savage deflation of the three preceding years and thus permit the permanent rehabilitation of the business and financial structure of the country, included three chief elements:

1. Establishment of a controlled economy, to reduce unemployment, stabilize industry and agriculture and maintain the price level.

2. Manipulation of the price level upward immediately through abandonment of the gold standard and monetary measures designed to establish a managed currency.

3. Relief from an unbalanced debt structure through refunding of farm and home mortgages

into bonds bearing a government guarantee as to interest.

A CONTROLLED ECONOMY

The most sweeping and lasting changes were embodied in the legislation for substituting government and cooperative control of industry and agriculture for the regime of free and unrestricted competition which had previously prevailed in the United States. The control program was embodied in the National Industrial Recovery Act, signed June 16, 1933, and the Agricultural Adjustment Act, approved May 12, 1933.

The National Industrial Recovery Act had two prime objectives. First, through fixing maximum hours and minimum wages and salaries, as well as through universal recognition of the collective bargaining principle, it sought to expand purchasing power and reduce unemployment. Secondly, each code of fair competition was to substitute cooperation for competition, and thus constitute a long step towards a cartel type of organization for American industry.

Agricultural Adjustment Act: The counterpart of the N.R.A., designed to give relief to agriculture, was the Agricultural Adjustment Act, signed by the President May 12, 1933. The philosophy underlying this legislation is the restoration of the prices of agricultural commodities to the parity of August, 1909, to July, 1914, and their maintenance at that level through control of future production to bring it into line with current consumption. Such equilibrium is to be obtained through reduction of acreage or of production, or both, of basic agricultural commodities such as wheat, cotton, field corn, hogs, rice, tobacco, milk and its products.

For the curtailment of production the farmer is to receive rental or bonus payments in such amounts as the Secretary of Agriculture deems fair and reasonable. These payments are to be financed through the imposition of processing taxes, to be paid by the processor and borne by the consumer. The tax rate is to be sufficient to yield the difference between the present average farm price of the commodity and the price needed to give the seller the same purchasing power he had during the base period. A compensating tax equal to the amount of the processing tax is to be imposed upon the importation of any article processed or manufactured wholly or in chief value from such commodity.

THE MANAGED CURRENCY PLAN

In his inaugural address, the President stated that he favored an "adequate but sound currency." It soon became evident that more emphasis would be laid on the adequacy and less on the soundness of the currency.

The Administration's currency policy had a two-fold objective: an immediate increase in prices, if possible to the 1926 level; and provision for maintenance of the future purchasing power of the dollar on an even keel. However, monetary management was not closely correlated with economic control, so that frequent shifts in emphasis from currency to economic control factors and the reverse marked the first year of the "New Deal."

The currency measures did not affect directly the banking situation, although it was hoped right along that bank credit expansion would result from new open market purchases of government bonds by the Reserve Banks. However, success of the managed currency plan, by improving the quality of bank loans and investments through establishing a higher price level, would give a measure of immediate relief to the banks.

The specific steps taken by the Administration in its managed currency campaign, after the reopening of the banks, were:

1. *The order against hoarding of gold, issued by the President, April* 5, 1933: It ordered all private individuals and corporations holding gold coin, gold bullion and gold certificates in amounts of over $100 to deliver it on or before

May 1, 1933, to a Federal Reserve or member bank. This order was regarded as an indication that the government would adopt a policy of currency depreciation, and therefore desired to prevent profits from the holding of gold.

2. *Gold embargo order of April* 20, 1933: Up to the issue of this order, the dollar moved only within narrow limits on the foreign exchange markets, for the banks could apply to the Treasury for gold to be exported. This order prohibited the earmarking of gold for foreign account, the export of gold coin, gold bullion or gold certificates from the United States, except for earmarked gold and a few other special cases, under license. In many respects this executive order constituted the definite act of the abandonment of the gold standard, in that it categorically prohibited the exportation of gold, with a few minor exceptions.

The same order authorized but did not direct the Secretary of the Treasury to investigate, regulate or prohibit transactions in foreign exchange. Although this was interpreted as the establishment of a foreign exchange control in the United States, however, as far as is known, very little use was made of this provision, for the Administration was primarily interested in the depreciation of the dollar, and any interference with the flight of capital would have obviated the depreciation policy.

3. *The Thomas Amendment to the Agricultural Act:* The provisions of the Thomas Amendment, Title II of the Agricultural Adjustment Act, authorized inflationary measures. They are permissive, not mandatory. The President is authorized to undertake any one, or all, of following four steps:

(*a*) To request the Federal Reserve System to conduct open market operations in obligations of the United States government or corporations in which the United States is a majority stockholder; in an aggregate sum of $3,000,000,000. If, as a result of these open market operations, the gold reserve of the Federal Reserve Banks should decline below the minimum fixed by law, the statutory graduated tax upon any deficiency in reserves is not to apply;

(*b*) If the Secretary of the Treasury should be unable to secure the assent of the Federal Reserve System to the above step, or if it should prove inadequate, to direct the Treasury to issue up to $3,000,000,000 in legal tender notes for the purpose of meeting maturing Federal obligations, to repay sums borrowed by the United States and for purchasing United States bonds or other interest bearing obligations of the United States. It was also provided that each year the total amount of such notes outstanding should be reduced by 5 per cent;

(*c*) To reduce by proclamation the gold content of the dollar by as much as 50 per cent; and

(*d*) To institute a bimetallic standard through the unlimited coinage of silver at a fixed ratio to gold.

The provision authorizing the purchase of government securities by the Reserve Banks caused little concern, since past experience had shown that a sharp increase in the excess reserve balances of the member banks does not necessarily result in an expansion in the volume of bank credit.

The bimetallism provision, the least likely of the four to have any effect, was merely a friendly gesture toward legislators representing the silver-producing states.

On the other hand, the authorization granted the President to order the issue of $3,000,000,000 of paper currency, coupled with the power to reduce the gold content of the dollar up to 50 per cent, created a great deal of concern and resulted in a sharp decline in the dollar in foreign exchange markets and in an increase in speculative activity. It was feared that if the other measures adopted by the Administration should not prove successful within a reasonable time, the President might actually have recourse to the issue of fiat money, and that once this easy road to "improvement in business" is taken it may be repeated, thereby leading to a debauch of the currency.

4. *The Abrogation of the Gold Clause:* The rapid depreciation of the dollar made it necessary to adopt measures concerning the gold clause provision which had been inserted in practically all obligations publicly offered in the United States during the past few decades. On June 5, the President signed a joint resolution of both houses voiding the gold clause on outstanding obligations. The resolution declared that all provisions contained in any obligation which gives the obligee the right to require payment in gold, or an amount in money of the United States equal to the current gold value, to be against public policy. It also prohibits the use of gold clauses in future contracts, and provides that every obligation heretofore or hereafter incurred, irrespective of any such clause, shall be discharged upon payment, dollar for dollar, in any coin or currency which at the time of payment is legal tender for public or private debts.

5. *Creating a market for newly mined gold in the United States:* Although the dollar had greatly depreciated, in the eyes of the law a paper dollar was still equivalent to a gold dollar and newly mined gold could be sold to the mints at first only at the legal parity of the dollar. Later on orders were issued whereby newly mined gold ore could be exported for refinement abroad. An executive order of August 29 authorized the Secretary of the Treasury to

receive newly mined gold in the United States on consignment for sale to (*a*) persons licensed to acquire gold for use in arts, industries or professions, or (*b*) by export to foreign purchasers. The sales were to be made at best prices obtainable in the free gold markets of the world.

This was the first step which took official cognizance of the depreciation of the dollar in relation to gold.

6. *Open market purchase of gold:* Up to October 26, the dollar fluctuated on foreign money markets primarily in response to demand and supply. Since the depreciation of the dollar was mainly the result of the flight of capital from the United States, it was obvious that its repatriation would cause a rapid appreciation of the dollar. After Germany left the Disarmament Conference and resigned from the League of Nations, Americans, fearing political upheavals in Europe, began to repatriate their capital, with the result that the dollar appreciated considerably. Inability of the French parliament to agree on means of reducing the rapidly growing deficit, with consequent fears of the abandonment of the gold standard there, accentuated this trend.

To obtain control over the movement of the dollar and to prevent its appreciation the President, in a radio address on October 22, announced that the Reconstruction Finance Corporation would buy newly mined gold in this country at prices independent of those of the free gold markets, and also buy and sell gold on the world's gold markets. So long as the Reconstruction Finance Corporation confined its activities to the purchase of newly mined gold at home, its gold price did not influence materially the movement of the dollar, and merely resulted in a situation where the price of gold measured in dollars was higher in the United States than abroad. Later on the Administration set up machinery to purchase gold abroad.

The new gold policy of the Administration, in contrast to the British Equalization Fund, was adopted not so much to control the fluctuation of the American currency, but rather to depress the value of the dollar in the international markets in the hope of raising domestic commodity prices.

MORTGAGE RELIEF

In addition to the previously described measures, the Administration took steps to reduce the debt burden on farms and small homes for the benefit of both debtor and creditor. These measures have a decided effect on the banking situation, in that banks have been enabled to convert certain types of frozen mortgages in their possession into marketable bonds enjoying a government guarantee of interest.

The Home Owners Loan Act, approved June 13, authorizes the Federal Home Loan Bank Board to establish a Home Owners Loan Corporation, with a capital of $200,000,000 to be subscribed entirely by the Treasury. This corporation has the power to issue $2,000,000,000 of tax exempt bonds bearing 4 per cent interest and maturing within eighteen years. The interest on the bonds is unconditionally guaranteed by the United States government.

The corporation may, up to June 13, 1936, take over mortgages on homes on record June 13, 1933, through the exchange for such mortgages of its own bonds up to an amount of $14,000 or 80 per cent of the value of the property as appraised by the corporation, whichever is the lower. The home owner in turn agrees to repay the loan to the corporation during a period of fifteen years, together with interest at a rate not exceeding 5 per cent per annum.

The corporation may also make cash loans to refund mortgages where holders refuse to exchange them for bonds of the corporation, and the home owners are unable to obtain loans from ordinary lending agencies. Such loans, however, may not exceed 40 per cent of the value of the property, and are to be authorized in fifteen years and bear not over 6 per cent interest per annum. In addition the corporation may grant cash loans to owners of homes not otherwise encumbered for the payment of taxes, assessments, necessary repairs and maintenance, but such loans may not exceed 50 per cent of the value of the property.

The Home Owners Loan Act is designed chiefly to refund outstanding mortgages on a favorable basis. It reduces debt burden of mortgagors and makes it possible for them to suspend principal payments for three years and to obtain additional loans for the payment of taxes and maintenance. The mortgagee, on the other hand, is offered a chance to convert a frozen mortgage into a marketable, interest-guaranteed bond. The marketability of the bond is enhanced by the fact that any person indebted to the corporation may pay his debt with such bonds at their face value.

The Agricultural Adjustment Act provides mortgage relief for farmers along the lines provided for home owners. The main provisions of Title II covering these points are:

(1) The Federal Land Banks are authorized to issue farm loan bonds up to $2,000,000,000, at an interest rate not in excess of 4 per cent, the interest to be guaranteed by the United States. The proceeds from these bonds shall be used for making new loans, or for purchasing mortgages or exchanging bonds for mortgages.

(2) The Federal Land Banks are authorized to buy first mortgages on farm lands situated

within their respective districts or to exchange farm loan bonds for duly recorded first farm land mortgages, at a price which shall not exceed the amount of the unpaid principal of the mortgages, or 50 per cent of the normal value of the land mortgaged and 20 per cent of the value of the permanent insured improvements thereon as determined by an appraisal, whichever is the smaller.

(3) Interest charged on loans made through National Farm Loan Associations shall not exceed 4½ per cent per annum, and no payment of the principal shall be required for five years if the borrower is not in default with respect to any other condition or covenant of his mortgage.

THE GLASS-STEAGALL ACT

A close study of the course of events at the special session of the Seventy-Third Congress, which met from March 9, 1933, to June 16, 1933, reveals that President Roosevelt did not himself favor enactment at the time of additional banking legislation after the passage of the emergency laws, at least until a new study of the situation could be made. Certain of his advisers, including Secretary of the Treasury Woodin, openly opposed further measures at that time.

Within Congress, however, support for more

permanent banking changes came from two sources—conservatives like Senator Carter Glass, who wanted to pass legislation which would bar the excesses of the boom years from occurring again and radicals who insisted upon a guarantee of bank deposits. In the closing days of the special session of Congress, these two groups combined, and probably gained added strength from individual members of Congress who were already feeling resentment against the President's general program but feared to express it openly at that time. As a result, the old Glass Bill, with a deposit guarantee feature of sweeping character added, was passed and, once adopted by Congress, was signed by the President with a superficial show of enthusiasm and praise.

The Banking Act of 1933, as the new measure is called, has effected the following important changes:

1. A guarantee of bank deposits is provided, presently to be described.

2. Participation of commercial banks in investment banking activities is curtailed through the segregation of security affiliates from banks, prohibition of underwriting of security issues by the banks themselves, additional limitations on investment in securities and real estate mortgages by the banks, and increased powers of the Federal Reserve Banks to limit expansion of security loans by member institutions.

3. Credit control powers of the Federal Reserve System are strengthened by giving the Federal Reserve Board direct jurisdiction over open market purchases of government bonds by the Federal Reserve Banks, and by increasing the Federal Reserve Banks' powers to regulate member banks' credit policies through the right to suspend their rediscounting privileges.

4. Member banks are forbidden to pay interest on demand deposits, thus reducing the incentive for making high-yield loans and investments and discouraging maintenance of large balances by interior banks with their city correspondents.

5. Brokers' loans for the account of others than banks are barred, as a measure to prevent a repetition of the large-scale financing of excessive speculation in defiance of the banking authorities, such as occurred in 1928 and 1929.

6. The Federal authorities are given authority to remove bank officers or directors, if their activities jeopardize the soundness of their institutions.

7. Holding companies which desire to vote stocks in national banks are placed under the regulation of the Federal Reserve Board, and are required to maintain liquid resources as a protection to depositors of the controlled institutions.

8. Investment banking houses may not engage

in a deposit banking business as long as they engage in wholesale or retail security activities.

9. Mutual savings banks are given the right to become members of the Federal Reserve System.

10. The Federal Reserve Board is given supervision over foreign relationships of any Federal Reserve bank.

THE GUARANTEE OF BANK DEPOSITS

While the bulk of the Banking Act of 1933 is concerned with the prevention of abuses of the kind which helped bring about the bank failure epidemic of 1930–33, the guarantee of bank deposits is designed to preclude a repetition of failures in large number, by protecting individual depositors against loss in any event, and so making runs unlikely.

It has long been argued by bankers that a deposit guarantee would not solve the banking problems, but would instead place a premium upon loose banking and drag down the strong banks with the weak in the event of a new depression. The failure of State guarantee of deposit schemes, tried in the Middle West, was cited also. Nevertheless, under the circumstances which prevailed in June, 1933, these objections went unheeded, and a modified guarantee of bank deposits became a fact.

The law sets up a Federal Deposit Insurance Corporation, to be managed by three directors, two appointed by the President and the third the Comptroller of the Currency. This agency, rather than the government, insures the deposits.

The funds for payments to depositors in insured banks that may be closed in the future are to be provided chiefly by the banks themselves, but a part of the money required is furnished by the Treasury and the Federal Reserve Banks. The Treasury makes an initial contribution of $150,000,000 for which it receives capital stock entitled to dividends. The Federal Reserve Banks subscribe to non-dividend stock a sum equal to one-half of their surplus, amounting to approximately $135,000,000. The balance of the funds needed to pay on deposits of failed banks is obtained from the participating banks. Stock held by the Treasury and the participating banks is entitled to yearly dividends up to 6 per cent or 30 per cent of the annual net earnings, whichever is greater, but there is no reason to believe that any material income will be available for distribution. Member banks of the Federal Reserve System subscribe to stock of the Bank Deposit Insurance Corporation a sum equal to one-half of one per cent of their total deposit liabilities. The right to subscribe to stock, and thus to enjoy the insurance of deposits provided by the law, is limited to institutions that satisfactorily pass an examination of their status by the Comptroller of the Currency or the Federal Reserve Board. Those that cannot meet this test by July 1, 1934, when the guarantee goes into effect, are compelled to leave the Reserve System. National banks are then placed in the hands of conservators or receivers.

Non-member banks which agree to join the Federal Reserve System by July 1, 1936, are permitted to enjoy the benefit of the deposit insurance provision in the interim. As a result, the deposit guarantee provision, by compelling all banks adhering to it to join the Federal Reserve System by July 1, 1936, does assure a partial unification of regulation of the American banking system.

The Federal Deposit Insurance Corporation guarantees deposits of participating banks in full up to $10,000; 75 per cent from $10,000 to $50,000, and 50 per cent above $50,000. Such sums are to be made available as expeditiously as possible in the form of deposits in a new national bank, which is to be formed to assume the insured deposit liabilities of the closed institution. It will also receive new deposits and otherwise perform temporarily the business of the closed bank. This new bank, if it obtains the requisite capital, may continue thereafter to operate as a regular banking institution. Otherwise, its assets may be transferred to some other banking institution, or it is liquidated through payments to depositors after two years. The assets of the closed bank are liquidated for the benefit of its depositors by the Federal Deposit Insurance Corporation. Closed state banks participating in the insurance fund are handled similarly, to the extent that state laws allow and state banking authorities give their approval.

Through forming new banks in this way to take over the activities of those that fail, the Federal Deposit Insurance Corporation will further curb the deflationary effect of future bank failures. Individual communities and entire areas will no longer suffer from complete disappearance of banking facilities, for new institutions will be organized as fast as others become defunct, once the plan is in full working order. Furthermore, the corporation is expected to make more orderly the liquidation of the assets of closed banks, since all such activities will tend to be concentrated in its hands.

The insurance corporation will expand its funds, in order to meet future claims for indemnification of depositors in closed banks, through the issuance of bonds up to three times its capital stock. Whenever the net debit balance in the deposit insurance account rises to $\frac{1}{4}$ of 1 per cent of all deposit liabilities of insured banks, the latter will be assessed such $\frac{1}{4}$ of 1 per cent, to replenish the funds of the corporation. No dividends may be paid by an insured bank on its own stock until all such assessments have been paid in full.

The corporation is authorized by law to open a temporary deposit insurance fund to cover the period from January 1 to July 1, 1934. All banks which satisfactorily pass an examination by their regulatory authorities are eligible to this temporary guarantee, on subscribing a sum equal to $\frac{1}{2}$ of 1 per cent of their deposits. The temporary insurance scheme covers in full deposits of not more than $2,500.

A NEW BANKING ERA

The establishment of the Federal Deposit Insurance Corporation, as well as the adoption of a comprehensive program of economic control designed to stabilize business conditions and prices, opens up a new era for American banking. For the time being, many of the structural defects of the pre-crisis banking system are retained, but in attenuated form. However, public opinion is coming gradually to accept the inevitability of changes which will tend both to expand branch banking and to unify banking control under federal jurisdiction.

In the meanwhile, the establishment of a

system of guarantee of bank deposits under which the strong banks will pay through the necessity of paying assessments, for the mistakes of weaker institutions has brought about a change in attitude. The metropolitan banker can no longer say that failures of small, interior institutions are of quite indirect and secondary concern to him. Through membership in the Federal Deposit Insurance Corporation, he must pay the piper in the long run. Accordingly, we find sound banking opinion in America now favoring actively a fundamental reorganization of the whole system.

One notable indication of this more social attitude of the large city bankers in the United States is the change in policy of the Association of Reserve City Bankers. This body for the past twenty-five years has shrouded its operations in secrecy. It has now come out, made public announcement of its existence and activities, and issues bulletins setting forth the need for fundamental banking reforms, as well as admitting sins of omission and commission on the part of the banking community which have contributed to the disasters of recent years. The Association of Reserve City Bankers may come to exercise the leading role in the preparation of future banking legislation which rightfully belongs to the American Bankers Association, and which the latter would not or could not use.

The number of commercial banks in the United States has been reduced by almost 50 per cent since the end of the war, chiefly through suspensions. The American public will not tolerate further transformation of its banking system through such a crude and cruelly painful process. The guarantee of deposits provided in the Banking Act of 1933 assures that, whatever happens, the rank and file of depositors will not be the sufferers. It provides an extended breathing spell, during which the banking community and the government can gradually develop a more modern banking system along lines that have proved successful in Great Britain and Canada, and yet adapted to special conditions which prevail in the United States.

IN CONCLUSION

A reorganization of the structure of American commercial banking along lines outlined above will tend to correct the conditions which made possible the catastrophic bank failure epidemic of the depression period. There remains the problem of good management, both for individual commercial banks and, more important, for our central bank—the Federal Reserve System. Reduction in the number of banks, closer supervision and wider publicity must be the chief factors that will have to be relied upon to help bring about better standards of management in individual institutions. The evolution of able central banking management, however, constitutes an even more difficult problem.

So fundamental and vital is central banking policy in modern economic life, that a nation cannot afford to have any but its most brilliant minds at the helm of such institutions. In several foreign countries, there is a wholesome tendency on the part of individual bankers to regard appointment to the direction of the central bank as the culmination of a life of service and accomplishment. In America, unfortunately, too many bankers in leading institutions regard a shift from a post with a commercial bank to one with a Federal Reserve bank as a demotion. Senior executives of not a few leading institutions would regard a suggestion that they resign their positions to become Governor or Chairman of the Board of a Federal Reserve bank as unthinkable. Perhaps the fact that the emoluments of Federal Reserve bank officials are small by comparison with salaries paid to higher executives of private banks helps explain this unfortunate attitude, although the Governor of the Federal Reserve bank of New York, the highest paid position in the system, receives $50,000 yearly.

The able, conservative banker represents one of the most valuable citizens any community can possess. Perhaps when public opinion honors him more for his ability and his conservatism rather than for his accumulation of and control over wealth, our banking leaders will show a more aggressive desire to contribute their time and efforts to general banking reform and effective central banking management, as well as to the safe conduct of their own individual institutions.

CHRONOLOGY OF THE BANKING PANIC

February 14—Michigan eight-day bank holiday decreed by Governor Comstock.

February 24—Governor of Maryland decrees a three-day holiday.

February 25—Indianapolis banks limit withdrawals to 5 per cent of deposits.

February 27—Pennsylvania, Ohio and Delaware enact legislation permitting individual banks to restrict deposit withdrawals.

March 1—Five states, including California, declare banking moratoria.

March 2—Seven additional states in the West decree bank holidays.

March 3—New York Federal Reserve Bank raises rediscount rate from 2½ to 3½ per cent. Announces money in circulation rose $732,000,000 for week ended March 1, a record rise.

March 4—New York and Illinois banks close, as well as Federal Reserve Banks. Other states follow suit, as well as security and commodity exchanges.

March 5—President Roosevelt decrees four-day bank holiday and embargo on gold shipments. Congress called in special session for March 9.

March 7—Secretary Woodin promulgates rules authorizing banks to make payments to cover needs for foods and medicines.

March 9—Congress passes emergency legislation giving President complete powers over banks and authorizing issue of Federal Reserve Bank notes without gold cover. Operation and reorganization of weak banks by conservators authorized.

March 11—Federal Reserve Banks reopen.

March 13—Licensed banks reopen in twelve Federal Reserve cities.

March 14—Licensed banks reopen in cities with recognized Clearing Houses.

March 15—Licensed banks reopen elsewhere throughout country.

June 16—Banking Act of 1933, with deposit insurance provisions, approved by President.

For Product Safety Concerns and Information please contact our EU representative GPSR@taylorandfrancis.com
Taylor & Francis Verlag GmbH, Kaufingerstraße 24, 80331 München, Germany

www.ingramcontent.com/pod-product-compliance
Ingram Content Group UK Ltd.
Pitfield, Milton Keynes, MK11 3LW, UK
UKHW022026061126
477531UK00002B/50

* 9 7 8 0 4 1 5 5 2 8 1 2 2 *